More Secret Stories of Disneyland

More Trivia Notes, Quotes, and Anecdotes

Jim Korkis

Theme Park Press
The Happiest Books on Earth
www.ThemeParkPress.com

Editor: Bob McLain
Layout: Artisanal Text

Cover Photo by Chris Bales

ISBN 978-1-68390-150-1
Printed in the United States of America
Theme Park Press | www.ThemeParkPress.com
Address queries to bob@themeparkpress.com

To the Disneyland designers who were mythical figures to so many of us and whose hard work, talent, creativity, and sometimes just dumb luck helped to make Walt Disney's dream come true for us all.

CONTENTS

Introduction

Everyone considers themselves a Disneyland expert, and with good reason.

Disneyland is the oldest of the Disney theme parks and has been in existence for over sixty years, so it is the most familiar. It is generally ranked as the highest attended Disney theme park each year and the one most frequently revisited. More people have spent time there and returned than any other Disney park.

Disneyland is the most documented of the Disney theme parks, with numerous books, magazine and newspaper articles, as well as websites recording almost everything about the place.

So, it seems like the height of hubris is to suggest that there still might be some "secrets" left to share. Yet, in 2017, rising to a challenge from my publisher, I was bold enough to produce a book of stories rarely told, never told, or told incorrectly in the past about the Happiest Place on Earth. Readers liked the book.

That should have been the end of the story because surely I had uncovered everything left to be found. Yet, while researching that first book, I re-examined the many interviews I have done over the years with Imagineers who worked on the park and the slowly decaying oddball newspaper and magazine clippings and fun facts that I had saved in my storage boxes and I thought I just might have enough for another volume.

Walt Disney World's Magic Kingdom and other Disney theme parks worldwide are patterned after Disneyland but are not identical. At best they are comparable, with several things sharing the same name being distinctly different.

Disneyland is unique. It was the first of its kind in outdoor entertainment. It was personally designed by Walt Disney who talked directly with the people building it and mingled with the guests and cast members to get their reactions, which prompted changes. Walt even had his own small apartment over the firehouse on Main Street, U.S.A. that is still maintained today.

Disneyland is ever-changing yet ever the same. Over the last six decades, it has experienced many additions and removals. But even today, with all of that, there is the feeling that this was where Walt lived and that his spirit still somehow remains.

For most people alive today, it is difficult to remember a time when there was no Disneyland and take for granted how its many innovations forever influenced outdoor entertainment and the hospitality industry.

Despite its limited space, Disneyland is always in a state of flux, with even a whole new land themed to the Star Wars movie franchise to debut shortly. While Disneyland's Pirates of the Caribbean attraction is reminiscent of the way it was when it first opened in 1967, significant changes have shifted the focus to the movie franchise with the addition of new figures and staging.

Everything in this book was in existence when the book was written, but that does not guarantee that in a short time some things will be hopelessly outdated or completely gone, making the book more of a document of ancient history than a brief glimpse at some hidden treasures.

Every effort has been made to give credit to the many talented people who remained anonymous, sometimes for decades, but whose contributions created the Happiest Place on Earth. However, the Disney company is notorious for incomplete documentation, so confirming facts was challenging; but every effort was made to do so from multiple sources.

I have also tried to avoid the most common "secrets" that are often repeated and are sometimes inaccurate, except in those instances where I could add new information or a new perspective. Often a "fun fact" that was correct when Disneyland first released the information is no longer true years later.

There are plenty of other reliable sources to help a fan find Hidden Mickeys or identify the names of the people on the upper windows of Main Street, U.S.A., so it didn't seem necessary for me to do so. I have also tried to remember that even though something may be common knowledge to me, it may still be a secret to others.

The purpose of this book is to record some of the information that is rarely if ever shared. Hopefully, it will present some surprising revelations not just for the most recent Disneyland fan but also for the veteran afficianado who calls the park their second home. This book really is nothing more than some trivia notes, quotes, and anecdotes to bring joy and information to those who love Disneyland and want to know a little bit more about it.

Please join me once again in re-discovering the often hidden magic and stories that transformed all of our lives and continues to take us to new Neverlands that enchant, enlighten, and entertain.

Jim Korkis
Disney Historian
April 2018

Main Street, U.S.A.

For an audience visiting Disneyland in 1955, the turn of the twentieth century with its typical small-town American main street was roughly a half century old, still fresh enough in people's memories or the many Hollywood movies set in that time period to bring a nostalgic smile at the thought of such things.

Disney Imagineer John Hench, who was involved in the design of Main Street including placing the different store façades right next to each other so that only four main buildings were needed to represent multiple businesses, stated:

> Main Street, of course, has the Victorian feeling, which is probably one of the great optimistic periods of the world, where we thought progress was great and we all knew where we were going.

> This form reflects that prosperity, that enthusiasm. Walt wanted to reassure people. There's some nostalgia involved, of course, but nostalgia for what? There was never a Main Street like this one. But it reminds you of some things about *yourself* that you've forgotten about.

Today, well over a century since its original physical existence in cities across the country, people still relate to the idea of a home-town main street and yearn for the aspects that it represented: small-town virtues, patriotism, friendliness, morality, security, family, small business, free enterprise, inventiveness, and progress, among other comforting values.

It is not Main Street as it actually was but as it should have been, being faithful to the blurred images of the past while removing such annoying imperfections as a funeral parlor, pool hall, dog pound, outhouses, and other contradictions to the story that Walt was trying to tell.

Guests boarding the horse-drawn streetcar or the steam train become enthusiastic and colorful extras in a much larger show enjoyed by others. On Main Street, everyone is part of the story of a bustling turn-of-the-century town with people shopping or rushing to other appointments or taking a moment to converse with friends and enjoy the general ambiance. It helps guests decompress from the real world and shifts their frame of mind into a happier mode.

Disney animator Ward Kimball remembered:

> [Walt Disney] was a man who loved nostalgia before it became fashionable. That's why so many of his pictures were set in that harmless period of American history because that was when he was a kid and happy.

MAIN STREET, U.S.A.

Attraction Posters

Since Disneyland is a living cinematic experience, it was natural that Walt Disney felt there should be strikingly dramatic attraction posters in the lobby of the park to entice guests to the newest attractions, exhibits, and restaurants, just like posters outside movie theaters sparked the interest of audiences coming to see the show.

Beginning in 1956, brightly silk-screened and framed attraction posters adorned the area outside and below the Main Street train station at the entrance of the park and also along other areas inside the park.

The bold use of color on these 36x54-inch posters is a vivid example of an art style popular in the 1950s, mixing angular design elements with bright pigments. The original series totaled seventeen designs including Peter Pan's Flight, Storybook Land, and the Santa Fe and Disneyland Railroad. The artwork for this series of posters has been credited to Disney artist Bjorn Aronson.

The early posters that captured the spirit of their attractions were intentionally designed with limited blocks of color to keep the silk-screen process uncomplicated. A separate matte (or stencil) was cut out for each color to be used and each color was then pulled by hand to complete the poster image. The Art of Animation poster only included four colors, but the more complex 20,000 Leagues Under the Sea poster had eleven colors.

Over the years, Disney Imagineers designed attraction posters including Claude Coats (Alice in Wonderland), Rolly Crump (Flying Saucers), and Mary Blair ("it's a small world"). Between 1956 and 1987, thirty-two different posters were created by Disney artists on large Masonite panels that were used as the model for the finished silk-screened print.

In the early years, Walt Disney himself approved each of the final posters before allowing them to be showcased at Disneyland in locations like the monorail beamway pylons outside the park, the famous Main Street entrance tunnels, and in the Penny Arcade. As the park evolved, certain attraction posters, like the one for the monorail (done by Paul Hartley), required updated images or text, and so new versions were made.

Some posters promoted upcoming attractions that never materialized, like the airboats ride that was to replace the Phantom Boats in 1957 in Tomorrowland.

While the attraction posters were only intended for display within Disneyland, over the years they were thought of as works of art and reproductions have been sold to the general public.

MAIN STREET, U.S.A.

Fort Collins Buildings

In many ways, Main Street, U.S.A. was inspired by Walt's own memories of growing up in Marceline, Missouri, in the early 1900s but with some significant differences to eliminate annoying imperfections.

It has been argued that a few architectural aspects from Marceline were used, like the distinctive style of the Zurcher building (a jewelry store in Marceline for seventy years, beginning in 1903) that bears a marked similarity to the Main Street Coca-Cola-sponsored Refreshment Corner building at the end of the street.

Recently, an antique, painted Coca-Cola advertisement was uncovered on a wall of a building next to the Zurcher building that Walt may have seen during his childhood there. However, it might also be argued that the style of architecture exhibited in the Zurcher building was common of buildings in other small-town main streets.

For years, many have been under the impression that City Hall on Main Street in Disneyland was based on a turn-of-the-century courthouse in Fort Collins, Colorado, which was the hometown of Imagineer Harper Goff, who supplied so much design work for Main Street. Goff himself claimed that was the case.

However, Imagineers have recently discovered that Disneyland's City Hall is actually based on the turn-of-the century Bay County Courthouse in Bay City, Michigan. The image was in a book about Victorian architecture in the Disney studio library also used as a source for the exterior of the Haunted Mansion.

Goff had mentioned that Walt wanted to recapture his memories of Marceline, but that "he decided to go with more two-story buildings to allow for additional storage space. That was what we had in Fort Collins where we had banks that looked like banks."

The Avery and Miller blocks, the old firehouse building, the former Linden Hotel, and the Union Pacific railroad station have all been considered possible inspiration for some of the façades on the Main Street buildings.

In addition, there were similarities with the storefronts on Jefferson Street, the First National Bank building, and buildings that had been torn down including Old Main, which burned down in 1970; the county's fourth courthouse, which was demolished in 1957; and Hottel House, which was razed to make way for a J.C. Penney and is now Old Town's Ace Hardware.

"These buildings were around when I was a kid," said Goff, who lived there from 1911 to around 1920. "They were my inspiration."

Roastie Toasties

The little character dolls turning a canister of popcorn connected to a faux steam pump are officially called Roastie Toasties. These popcorn animation dolls have been a part of Disneyland as far back as 1955.

However, their history goes back to the late 1800s (in keeping with the time period of Main Street, U.S.A.) when they originally decorated peanut-roasting machines produced by Charles Cretors & Company and were called Toasty Roasty Men.

They were meant to attract and amuse customers and were popular at the 1893 Columbian Exposition in Chicago where Walt's father had worked in constructing the pavilions. The little figures started appearing on popcorn carts in the 1920s and Walt remembered them.

The Disneyland popcorn carts themselves were called "Cretors" and used some actual Cretors' parts and roasters. However, the design of the Disneyland cart itself seems to have been a mixture of elements from what were known as the #1 and #2 wagons first produced from 1902 to 1911 but available into the 1920s.

The earliest Disneyland wagons had a thinner, more delicate chassis and finer spoke wheels. Some deluxe options were included, like the addition of a canopy that wouldn't have appeared on the original Cretors.

These original Disneyland wagons were replaced in May 1975 by seven variations on a standard design by Imagineer Tom Yorke. The variations were primarily different wheel types or differences in the trim.

These wagons' detailed scroll work and trimmings and graphics were not hand-painted but were done using intricate screen-printed decals. The original wagons were hand-painted and lettered. One of the original wagons was kept and used as a backup for several years. The next generation larger model was introduced into the park in 2015.

In the early days of Disneyland, the Roastie Toasties were all clown figures. Gradually, they evolved so that they were themed to the lands where their carts were located.

Those characters include a train conductor, an undertaker, the Abominable Snowman, the Rocketeer, a bearded frontiersman wearing a Davy Crockett coonskin cap, clowns, two Dapper Dans with pin-striped pants, and seasonal characters like Oogie Boogie from *Nightmare Before Christmas* and Santa Claus appear during the Yuletide season, replacing some of the more familiar Roastie Toasties.

Smellitzer

The distinctive smells in many of the attractions, from the orange scent in Soarin' to a whiff of sea air in Pirates of the Caribbean to the aroma of vanilla coming from the Main Street Bakery, are the result of a Disney technology called a smellitzer.

It was named by its creator, Imagineer Bob McCarthy, who first developed it for use at Epcot, originally for the smell of smoke in the Roman ruins scene in Spaceship Earth and the appropriate smells for The Land pavilion. Technically it is called a scent-emitting system.

The smellitzer operates like an air cannon, aiming the scent up to 200 feet across a room toward an exhaust system. Guests traveling on the moving vehicles pass through the scene as the appropriate scent drifts across their path. Regulated by computer, the scent can be triggered for a fresh aroma just prior to each vehicle's arrival.

The smellitzer uses a series of pumps and vents to launch the smells up to 200 feet at just the right second. Then an exhaust system sucks the odor out of the area before it interferes with the next sensory experience.

McCarthy said:

> Back in the 1950s, [film producer] Mike Todd developed a process called "smell-a-vision." The idea was to release certain scents into the theatre as the visual counterpart was shown on the screen.

McCarthy, who worked with Todd on the project, explained:

The main problem was that odors tended to linger in the air. After a while they all blended together. We couldn't get the scents in and out of the theatre quickly enough.

The situation was different at a Disney theme park because the guests would be moving quickly through the area and there were no additional scents overlaying the original. Imagineers also learned how to regulate the strength or intensity of the odors used.

McCarthy filed the patent on September 20, 1984 and it was approved on July 29, 1986. The abstract described it as:

> A system for emitting, in sequence, a plurality of different scents; includes a plurality of holders for scent-bearing chips; a mechanism for propelling these scents from a system; a mechanism for conveying, selectively, any desired scent holder into operative relation with the propelling mechanism; and a mechanism for actuating the propelling mechanism to propel scent from any desired scent holder in response to a programmed, predetermined sequence of scents of predetermined duration.

C.K. Holliday

On the morning of August 8, 1953, Walt reviewed the site map that Imagineer Marvin Davis was working on for Disneyland, picked up a No. 1 carbon pencil, and drew a triangle around the plot of land to indicate where he wanted a railroad to be located, explaining:

> I just want it to look like nothing else in the world. And it should be surrounded by a train.

The *C.K. Holliday* was the first engine to be built and was named after Cyrus Holliday, the founder of the Atchison & Topeka Railroad, the predecessor of the Santa Fe Railroad, since the Disneyland Railroad was originally sponsored by Santa Fe up until 1974. It was 5/8th scale, although the cab was 3/4th scale to allow sufficient room for the engineer and fireman.

The construction was based directly on the drawings Imagineer Eddie Sargeant had done for the 1/8th scale *Lilly Belle* locomotive that was part of Walt Disney's backyard miniature railroad, the Carolwood Pacific. Those designs had been based on the original blueprints of the Central Pacific Railroad's No. 173 from 1872.

The Disneyland engine was identical to the smaller version except for the addition of a Westinghouse air compressor to supply braking and the fact that the wood cab on the miniature was natural color while the *C.K. Holliday* was painted a bright red.

The *Holliday* was built on the soundstage at the Disney studio in Burbank. Dixon Boiler Works constructed the boiler and Wilmington Iron Works cast the wheels and frame. Everything else was fashioned in the studio machine shop under the supervision of its chief machinist, Roger Broggie, often considered the first Imagineer. Everything was assembled in the new roundhouse building at Disneyland.

Just the engine alone had cost $40,511. In 1958, the three cattle cars and gondolas that the train pulled were re-designed with side-facing bench seating to better view the newly opened Grand Canyon Diorama, and red-and-white striped awnings were added as well.

At the same time the *E.P. Ripley* was built and was mechanically identical to the *Holliday*, but the exterior was modeled after the Baltimore & Ohio Railroad's No. 774 built in 1887. It was named after Edward Ripley, the first president of the Atchison, Topeka & Santa Fe Railway. This would be the last locomotive to be custom built for Disneyland. All others were restored versions of actual narrow-gauge engines.

MAIN STREET, U.S.A.

The Ghost on the Fred Gurley

The *Fred Gurley* came into service in 1958 and was named after the man who was then the president of the Atchison, Topeka & Santa Fe Railway.

The first two engines (*E.P. Ripley* and *C.K. Holliday*) had been built from scratch at a cost of nearly $50,000 each. The *Fred Gurley* was re-built at the Disney studio and even after all of the needed work, the total cost was $37,061—significantly less than the previous engines.

The *Fred Gurley* was originally built by the Baldwin Locomotive Works of Philadelphia in August 1894 and spent much of its time carrying sugar in Louisiana.

The years of hauling sugar in humid weather had taken its toil on the little engine and much of it was rusted and had wood rot. However, some important things were salvageable, such as the frame, wheels, cylinders, and domes, as well as the bell that still rang clear despite decades of grime and soot.

Before the engine was later completely rebuilt in 2006, it was the oldest engine on the route. Some claim it was the most haunted of the locomotives that operated at Disneyland. Many said that on quiet, warm nights a ghostly engineer could be seen riding in the cab.

The claim was accompanied by stories that in the evening, as the *Fred Gurley* pulled out of the Mickey's Toontown station and rolled past "it's a small world," the original bell on the locomotive would slowly rock back and forth and then ring loudly even though it was not touched by anyone riding in the cab.

It was not a bumpy or uneven stretch of track but actually very smooth and the *Fred Gurley* was the only engine to have this effect happen. At least one engineer has claimed that he heard the bell ring on its own even when it was stopped at a station.

The first chief engineer at the park when it opened in July 1955 was Harley Ilgin who had previously worked for the Santa Fe. Ilgin suffered a fatal heart attack one day as the train rolled through the Grand Canyon Diorama.

It was shortly after his death that stories of the bell ringing on its own began to be shared. It was believed that the tobacco spitting (with Walt's permission) chief engineer was still on the job and just letting others know of his presence.

MAIN STREET, U.S.A.

Lincoln's Gettysburg Address

Lincoln scholar Ralph Newman had been brought in by Walt Disney to help James Algar script the Great Moments with Mr. Lincoln show for the 1964–65 New York World's Fair that was then transplanted to Disneyland.

Newman told Disney historian Paul Anderson:

> We both agreed completely that we would not have Lincoln giving the Gettsyburg Address because everybody would be anticipating that, and that would be kind of anti-climatic.

Walt Disney said in 1964:

> When we set out to select the speeches and writing for the monologue in the show, we decided to bypass the Gettysburg Address even though its poetic qualities and poignant message are unexcelled. Because it is so familiar to nearly every American, we felt that it would not contribute significantly to our purpose—an in-depth, fresh presentation of Lincoln's principles, ideals, and philosophies.

On July 17, 2001, the attraction was drastically changed to include the famous speech. In December 2009, it was revised again to return to the original speech.

Where did the voice track of actor Royal Dano performing the Gettsyburg Address come from if it was not part of the original presentation, especially since Dano had already passed away?

Algar also produced and wrote the Buena Vista LP record (BV-3981) entitled *Walt Disney Presents Great Moments with Mr. Lincoln* that was released in connection with the New York World's Fair. In addition to the actual presentation (which was later performed at Disneyland), Algar directed Royal Dano in recording other Lincoln speeches including the Gettysburg Address.

The Imagineers uncovered these recordings when the attractions at both Disneyland and Walt Disney World were updated.

Walt was insistent that he wanted "not an actor's voice, but the real voice" as could be best re-created. Dano had done a five-part episode show for the *Omnibus* television series in 1952 written by James Agee where he played Lincoln and received laudatory reviews for capturing the homespun nature of the man.

Of course, at the time there was no one alive who had actually heard Lincoln speak and there were no audio recordings. Research was done based on written contemporary accounts and knowledge of speech patterns from the rural areas where Lincoln grew up, but Dano's interpretation has always seemed "emotionally right" even if scholars have argued that it may not be completely accurate in all respects.

Refreshment Corner

When Disneyland opened in July 1955, at the end of Main Street just at the beginning of the hub was a quick-service restaurant called Refreshment Corner that was sponsored by Coca-Cola. It is more commonly referred to by guests as just Coke Corner.

Originally, both Coca-Cola and Pepsi-Cola were served at Disneyland, but in 1982, Coke made arrangements to become the sole provider and has remained so for over the last thirty-five years. Coca-Cola was invented by John Pemberton back in 1886, making it an appropriate offering on Main Street.

According to the official Disney description:

> Take a break on the shaded patio and listen to the tinkling of ivories of our ragtime piano player. Enjoy crowd-pleasing American classics like hot dogs, sourdough chili bowls, soft pretzels, desserts, and fountain drinks. Hosted by Coca-Cola.

The Refreshment Corner sells enough hot dogs in one year to encircle Disneyland 36 times.

For many years, Rod Miller could be found playing ragtime and Disney tunes on the upright piano at the Refreshment Corner throughout the day and night, often until midnight. Miller taught himself how to play piano. Moving to California in 1966, he performed at Shakey's Pizza and Northwood's Inn. An entertainment executive from Disney caught his act at the Maple Leaf Club and offered him a job at Disneyland.

He performed at the Refreshment Corner from 1969 to 2006 when continuing problems with his back forced him to retire from the grueling schedule.

While performing he met a talented young pianist named Alan Thompson who became his protégé. Together they developed "four-hand piano" ragtime which they sometimes performed at the restaurant.

Above the entranceway there is a series of alternating red and white lightbulbs representing the iconic colors of Coca-Cola. However, because of the shape of the area and the bulbs being placed in two different orders, their spacing resulted in an odd number so, in theory, there was not enough space to complete the pattern.

It was Walt Disney who suggested painting one bulb half white and half red to keep the color changes consistent. It's not ordinary paint. It's a high-temp translucent coating developed for specialty lamps. If you try to use regular oil or latex paint (which is opaque), no light will come through, and it will burn off.

Adventureland

Walt Disney described Adventureland as:

> Here is adventure. Here is romance. Here is mystery. Tropical rivers silently flowing into the unknown. The unbelievable splendor of exotic flowers...the eerie sound of the jungle...with eyes that are always watching.

In the 1955 Disneyland guide map, it was described as:

> Those romantic, tropical far-away places that all of us yearn to see, await your visit in Adventureland. A Tahitian trading post provides an exotic threshold for this wonder-world of Nature's own design. Here you'll marvel at the display of tropical flowers, birds, fish and native handicraft gathered from all latitudes.

Some of the Tiki carvings at the entrance are the originals carved by Imagineer Harper Goff in his garage and have not only survived the weather for decades but the re-adjustment of their positions when the bridge was widened in 1994.

The definition of adventure has changed over the decades from that vaguely cinematic amalgamation of different exotic and remote areas around the world. Today, the land is home to such classic adventurers as Tarzan and Indiana Jones.

In fact, the introduction of the Indiana Jones Adventure in 1995 impacted the Jungle Cruise so that it became more of a 1930s outpost and the launches re-themed to be more realistic looking. At one point, there were plans for the Jungle Cruise as well as the Disneyland Railroad to venture inside the Indiana Jones Adventure.

The Jungle Cruise was so iconic that in December 1999, the Disneyland Hotel introduced a remote-controlled attraction called Safari Adventure that used tokens where guests could guide miniature versions of the original candy-striped motor launches through a number of colorful experiences. It was built by Thola Productions of Laguna Hills, California.

Unlike the actual Jungle Cruise, guests could pilot their craft behind Diswaytada Falls, pass a gorilla on a suspension bridge, or take a shortcut through a rocky island tunnel that triggers an explosion. At one point, there was even a tiny elephant that squirts water from its trunk to help put out a fire on one of the launches.

With the most recent renovation of the Disneyland Hotel, Safari Adventure closed in July 2010. Today, Tangaroa Terrace and Trader Sam's Enchanted Tiki Bar are adjacent to the old site. In 2009, parody composer "Weird Al" Yankovic wrote and recorded a song titled "Skipper Dan" about a failed actor who ended up as a guide on the Jungle Cruise.

Harper Goff: The Jungle Cruise

In a 1988 interview, Imagineer Harper Goff stated:

> After being impressed with John Huston's film *The African Queen* (1951) the attraction was changed to be primarily an adventure ride set in Africa. I couldn't get Walt to go see *The African Queen*, so I ordered a print in for him to watch at the studio.
>
> Animation [of mechanical figures] wasn't very good back then, but I told Walt that like in the film the animals could be partly hidden. We could have elephants hiding behind trees so they would only have to move a little bit. The other animals would be partially hidden, too.
>
> At the time, Walt didn't want the animals to be electrically operated because he said a kid would stick his hand in the water some day and accidentally get electrocuted. So we had motors hydraulically operated, but then we had problems when the water pressure varied as it often did in those days.
>
> Bob Mattey proved that we could safely run the ride electronically and Walt was happy about that. It provided more of a consistency.
>
> I didn't want Walt with me the first time I went through the path to see all the boo-boos. I removed the bottom of one of the boats and strapped it on to the top of a Jeep and went along the route before the water was filled in. We had to correct some of the curves but that was about it. It all seemed to work pretty smoothly.
>
> It was the only ride that ran without breaking the whole of opening day. I was pretty proud of that. Walt asked

me to accompany the press through the river ride. I'd finally get through with one large batch of reporters and then along came another large group. It was wall-to-wall press.

And the press had a skeptical view of Walt's idea of an educational park. Remember the Jungle Cruise was supposed to be like the True-Life Adventure pictures and tell people all these facts.

The models for the animals on the Jungle Cruise were sculpted by Chris Mueller who used clay to build figures for molds that were later cast in fiberglass.

Then Bob Mattey, who later created the shark for *Jaws* (1975), was responsible for installing a mixture of spring steel, rubber, and flexible tubing on rocker arms or hinged joints that were operated by cams and levers connected to electric motors.

Marc Davis & John Hench:
Jungle Cruise Elephants

In 1998, Marc Davis told me:

> There was no real humor on the Jungle Cruise and I wanted to put some in there. I put in the elephant pool [1962] and I did idea sketches of what the elephants would look like and what they would be doing.

> The original attraction they had done the big African elephant so I was pretty sure they could make an elephant. We got marvelous sculpture done on the elephants. You can't compliment Blaine Gibson enough for supervising the doing of these things.

> I went down there with Walt after putting all these elephants in there. I knew there was no way anybody could go through that ride and see all these elephants, but Walt thought that was great. He felt people would ride it again just to see what they had missed.

Imagineer John Hench told me in 1995:

> We create a world people can escape to...to enjoy for a few brief moments...a world that is the way they would like to think it would be.

> The Jungle Cruise is a good example of what I'm talking about. It began as an adaptation from our True-Life Adventure films. We created an attraction where all the things that you might see on a jungle river journey actually do happen. The truth of the matter is, you could probably spend two years on a real journey like that before you'd see everything we included.

Later, in selected Jungle Cruise scenes, we further enhanced the entertainment value by adding a touch of fantasy here and there. Take the elephant bathing pool, for example. Our guests know that real elephants wouldn't lurk under the water and then rise up to squirt the boat.

And they know that a real herd of elephants wouldn't be quite so happy with a strange boat in their midst. Real elephants would have either retreated defensively into the jungle or smashed the boat to pieces. But again, we've programmed in a kind of utopian realism, added a touch of fun and fantasy, and the guests love it and accept it.

The combination of the natural appearance of the sculpted rock formations, the planted jungle landscape, and the dramatic staging all make the guests accept the presence of a jungle in the midst of a former orange grove beside a major freeway. It never occurs to them to question it at all.

John Hench: Tiki Room Memories

In a 1996 interview, Imagineer John Hench stated:

> Some Disneyland ideas changed from their initial concept. The Tiki room, for instance, was supposed to be a Polynesian restaurant. I had ordered tables, I had bought all the furniture. I visualized the entire thing: décor, show, dining area, all simultaneously in a cross-shaped room with four wings and a service center in the shared central area to not obstruct the view from any table in each wing.
>
> And Walt was listening one morning to a rehearsal of the show, and he said: "If we get rid of the tables, how many more people can we get in here?" So I took the tables out, arranged the chairs in a certain way, etc. ... And he said: "That's what we gonna do. I'll handle the man who was to operate the restaurant [Stouffers]. So we can make a show out of it."
>
> But the show was all done, and it was a show that didn't have a curtain riser. It was supposed to start up very gradually while people were eating. Walt's idea was that as soon as the people who were dining got through their main course...when they got into the dessert...this music that was supposed to only come from speakers like in any restaurant. But then one bird will start to do a little jazz scat thing, and another bird will start to answer. And people would say: "Something is going on here! What is this?" and the show would have come very gradually.
>
> In the first version, we had to pretend that he birds were asleep. Somebody came in saying, "Hey, wake up, wake up!" And we started the show that way which was very

bad. I was always embarrassed about this. Because you can't design a show for one operation and then make a change so radically.

I set an elaborately carved fountain in the central area whose jet of water reached eight feet in the air. The engineer who reviewed my illustration said it couldn't be done, that the column of water would break in the middle. I asked Roger Broggie if we could use a hollow glass tube and he said that if the the hole was deep enough to recess the tube and there was a lifting machine, it might work. We did it and the overflowing water hid the glass tube completely.

Tiki Room Song

Songwriting team Richard and Robert Sherman did not just provide memorable songs for the Disney films but also for the theme parks including the first original song for a Disneyland attraction, "The Tiki, Tiki, Tiki Room." As Richard Sherman told me:

> Walt's secretary called us up one day and asked us to come over to Stage 3 at the studio. We found ourselves in a big room set up in the middle of the stage with four walls, dozens of exotic birds, and hundreds of tropical flowers. Sitting on bridge chairs, we saw the birds sing and the flowers croon and Tikis on the wall come to life. It was the strangest thing in the world.

> Walt said, "It's a great show, but nobody knows what it is all about." Two years earlier we had written a lengthy calypso song to cover a lot of boring footage showing how the Disney crews had carted tons and tons of equipment to Tobago to film *Swiss Family Robinson*. It was a crazy song, but it tied all the footage together for the TV show. So we suggested an articulate parrot to sing a song to set up the show to a similar calypso beat. Walt added, "Instead of one parrot emcee, we'll have four with French, Spanish, German, and Irish accents."

As early as May 1962, composer George Bruns conducted a twenty-four piece orchestra and over a dozen vocalists in recording music for the attraction including the harp solo as the fountain magically rises.

The background whistles and bird calls were supplied by Maurice Marcelino, Purvis Pullen, and Clarence

Nash, all of whom had all provided a variety of avian sounds professionally for decades. Their work was supplemented by Beverly Ford and Dorothy Lloyd. Singer Norma Zimmer is the voice of the orchid whose solo triggers the Tiki chanting. The ladies on the bird mobile were Sue Allen, Sue Lewis, Sally Sweetland, Betty Wand, and Jeanne Gayle. Wally Boag, Fulton Burley, Thurl Ravenscroft, and Ernie Newton as the parrot emcees were the leads on the title song.

The song "Hawaiian War Chant" was originally going to be sung with English lyrics, but it was decided to keep it in its original language. The exit song was going to be "Colonel Bogey March" (from the movie *Bridge on the River Kwai*) before being replaced by "Heigh-Ho" from *Snow White and the Seven Dwarfs*.

Little Man of Disneyland

Western Printing and Lithographing had a long relationship with Disney beginning in 1933. Western produced material for Disney comic books, sticker books, coloring books, and the iconic Little Golden Books.

In 1955, the company released three Little Golden Books devoted to Disneyland: *Disneyland on the Air*, *Donald Duck in Disneyland*, and *Little Man of Disneyland*. They were all written by Annie North Bedford, a pseudonym used by Jane Werner Watson, one of the original editors of Little Golden Books. The last book was illustrated by Dick Kelsey, a Disney animation director who assisted with the design of Disneyland.

The story was of a leprechaun named Patrick Begorra who lived comfortably in the roots of a tree in an orange grove in Anaheim that was destined to become Disneyland. He is not too happy about this event and prepares to cause trouble until Mickey Mouse, Donald Duck, and Goofy take him on a helicopter ride to the Disney studio in Burbank to see the blueprints and drawings.

Patrick agrees to let them build the theme park as long as he can still live there in a wee small house in a secret location. In the book, Donald talks to the leprechaun about his new house near the Jungle Cruise so readers assumed the home was in Adventureland. The book invited readers to search for that hidden home and they did.

Some have claimed that the book's popularity resulted in Walt having a tiny door and windows constructed in the base of a tree so guests could peer inside and see tiny furniture. Later, the hole was filled up with concrete. Disneyland landscaper Bill Evans occasionally filled holes in trees with concrete.

Former Disney archivist Dave Smith has debunked the story of the home multiple times and claims it is an example of the Mandella Effect, or false memories. No photos or documentation exist of this supposed hidden hideaway.

However, in August 2015, as part of the events of the D23 Expo and a special reprint of the book reissued for the celebration, it was revealed that there is now a tiny home for the leprechaun, based exactly on Kelsey's illustration of it in the book, at the base of the tree under the sign for the Indiana Jones attraction. The pebbled Welcome Mat in front has the letters "PB" and there is a stove-pipe chimney sticking out to the side of the door.

Tony Baxter: Tarzan's Treehouse

Imagineer Tony Baxter was in charge of transforming the iconic Swiss Family Treehouse to Tarzan's Treehouse. He recalled:

> I don't think we should ever take out anything that is regarded as a "classic" or even a "semi-classic" for that matter unless whatever we were going to do was the same quality if not better than the original we were replacing.

> I think all of us who love Disneyland liked having the Swiss Family Treehouse there, but the reality was that people would walk by and smile and love hearing the music but would just keep walking. Disneyland is so tight for space that you need to have everything pulling its share. The attraction had dropped from 1,200 to approximately 300 guests per hour and yet there was an hour-and-a-half line for Indiana Jones and a thirty minute wait for Pirates just minutes away.

> It was around May of 1998 when I got to see a rough cut of [the animated feature] *Tarzan* and I just felt it was extraordinary. The last three animated films were not appealing to me and I didn't connect with them like I did with the Disney classics. I found a great depth of emotion in the film and that you cared about this character. It was centered around home and family just like the Swiss Family Treehouse.

> It seemed obvious that if Jane was going to stay in the jungle with Tarzan and there was this treehouse that his parents had built that it was where they would set up their home. When we talked to the co-directors, Kevin

Lima and Chris Buck, they kind of smiled because they had the same idea if there was to be a sequel to the film.

Today, people just aren't as familiar with the *Swiss Family Robinson* movie. People don't see the film anymore and think they want to visit it at Disneyland. It took on a life of its own as this Disney attraction and we felt we could increase attendance if it was somehow connected to something Disney that the current generation knows and loves.

My biggest fear is we would make these changes and the same 300 people an hour would still just visit it. When we started hitting 1,200 or more almost immediately and they had to erect a little queue for the bridge, I knew we had made the right choice.

Tarzan's Treehouse

In February 1999, Disneyland closed the Swiss Family Treehouse that had opened in November 1962 as a reference to Disney's live-action film *Swiss Family Robinson* (1960) that featured a similar tree. Imagineers studied the gnarled roots of the mammoth Moreton Bay Fig Tree planted in the 1800s by Anaheim horticulturist Tim Carroll to aid in authentically creating details of the Disneyland tree. It reopened on June 23, 1999, as Tarzan's Treehouse.

Landscaper Bill Evans had dubbed the original tree *Disneyodendron Semperflorens Grandis* which means "large, ever-blooming Disney tree," and the new version retains that same designation.

The giant artificial tree received a massive makeover including 6,000 replacement vinyl leaves as well as additional foliage and a new suspension bridge entrance from a new neighboring tree that helps obscure the end of Adventureland and New Orleans Square.

The idea was not just to remove all the Swiss Family items and replace them with Tarzan items but to make it definitively Tarzan's tree. Disney raised the main trunk of the tree by ten additional feet, held it there in place, welded in a new section, and had to get structural approval before they could continue. The initial modeling was done on computer to adjust the look before it was connected.

The tree weighs 150 tons, features 450 branches, and is anchored 42 feet into the ground. The treehouse features several rooms in the branches that are connected by a series of ramps and winding stairs. These rooms feature key scenes from the film.

In the room where Jane is drawing Tarzan, one of the books on the table is a copy of *Swiss Family Robinson*.

The music is by Phil Collins who supplied the songs for the movie. Show writer Bruce Gordon took it and made it cyclic so that it could repeat naturally without ending and starting over. It is instrumental without vocals to establish the same tone as the movie.

The background music that plays throughout the tree and the love scene between Jane and Tarzan were newly recorded by Andy Belling because in the original film they were either too powerful or with vocals and so wouldn't be easy to repeat.

In the campsite play area, the teapot and chipped teacup on the left are Mrs. Potts and Chip from the animated feature *Beauty and the Beast*. They had made a cameo appearance at Jane's tea party at the camp in the animated film *Tarzan*.

Swiss Family Robinson Tributes

In the conversion of the Swiss Family Treehouse to Tarzan's Treehouse, the Imagineers included some significant tributes to the original attraction and their re-use also saved money while adding to the overall detail.

The blue ore on the entrance staircase is from the original side fence. The lower railing pieces on the entrance staircase are from the original treehouse's railings.

The ship's bell is from the Swiss Family's library. The sea shell planter is originally from the main room.

The chest in Sabor's area is originally from the boy's room. The chest in Kala's room was originally found in the parent's room. The paneled side wall is in the exact same place. The organ used to sit in front of it.

One remaining branch of the original leaves still exists hidden under the final room but is only visible from below. The hanging barrel is from the original tree.

The curious baby elephant known as "Li'l Squirt" is from the Jungle Cruise's sacred bathing pool.

A rope ladder on the mast is the original bucket chain from the water conveyor system. Many of the new orchids are planted in buckets from the original treehouse's water conveyor system.

Several of the lamp posts are from various locations within the original attraction. Many of the light fixtures are from the original treehouse.

Originally, Imagineering had plans to upgrade the treehouse including more kinetics for children to interact with. A lot of expensive nautical antiques were purchased for this new concept and got absorbed into Tarzan's Treehouse.

The famous "Swisskapolka" composed by Buddy Baker for the film and later at the original attraction is now playing on the Victrola gramophone near the base camp.

Imagineer Tony Baxter told historian Rick West:

> We took the "Swisskapolka" and converted it over to a very scratchy, "used" 78 rpm record version and it's performed on the gramophone. We're actually using a tiny little speaker that is using the horn in the same way that the music would be reproduced authentically. We thought that was appropriate because if the Swiss family happened somewhere in the mid-1850s, the sheet music could have easily been recorded around the turn of the century, when Tarzan was taking place. There *was* a gramophone in the [animated] movie at the camp so all of this kind of worked out real nice, and we have our homage to what is truly a wonderful piece of Disney music!

Dole Whip

A cult following for a soft-serve frozen dessert created by the Dole Food company known as Dole Whip has created such a frenzy in Disney theme park fans that many suspect the treat is only available at Disney. It is not.

It has been served for decades at the Dole Plantation three miles north of Wahiawa, Hawaii, but in recent years, thanks to the ease in creating it, a variety of popular venues now offer it, from sporting events to zoos to state fairs and other amusement venues. Outside of Disney, vendors are strongly encouraged to use the term Dole Soft Serve instead.

"Disney has literally created Dole Whip devotees," stated Jamie Schwartz of Kent Precision Foods Group that licenses the product. "Disney built [up] the brand."

When Walt Disney's Enchanted Tiki Room opened in June 1963, it was sponsored by United Airlines promoting its flights to Hawaii. In 1976, Dole Food took over sponsorship and opened up a food and beverage stand at the entrance to the attraction called the Tiki Bar.

Karlos Siqueiros, Disneyland's concept manager of Food Operations, recalled that in the beginning the little stand only sold pineapple juice and pineapple spears:

> Pineapple juice had always been served at the Tiki stand, but we didn't have anything to add to it literally until the Dole Whip came in.

The soft-serve pineapple dessert can also be purchased as a "float" with pineapple juice or as a swirl of pineapple and vanilla. While most Disney fans associate the term "Dole Whip" with pineapple soft serve, it also comes in several other flavors like orange, strawberry, lemon, raspberry, and mango.

In 1997, Kent Precision Foods Group in St. Louis, Missouri, began to license the Dole Whip product. While it used to contain a dairy derivative, in 2013 the formula was changed and it became certified as vegan and gluten free. They sell Dole Whip Mix, a dry powder, online. To make it just like at Disney, all that needs to happen is to add water and pour it into a home soft-serve ice cream machine.

It is estimated that park guests at Disneyland and Walt Disney World consume 1.4 million Dole Whips each year. (Disneyland consumes a minimum of 600,000.) It is not served at any of the other Disney theme parks worldwide. At the Aulani Resort in Hawaii, it is offered at the Lava Shack.

Frontierland

On July 5, 1955, Walt Disney approved the following wording for a plaque to be installed at the entrance of Frontierland:

> Here we experience the story of our country's past...the colorful drama of Frontier America in the exciting days of the covered wagon and the stage coach...the advent of the railroad...and the romantic riverboat. Frontierland is a tribute to the faith, courage and ingenuity of the pioneers who blazed the trails across America.

While Walt read similar words during the televised opening of the land on July 17, 1955, the plaque was never installed. However, there was a plaque at the entrance to Frontierland in 1955, given to Walt by the American Humane Association in July 1955, which reads:

> To Walt Disney in Recognition of Outstanding Assistance and Cooperation in Extending Humane Ideals To Peoples Throughout the World from the American Humane Association.

The plaque now sits atop a rock pedestal near the base of a flagpole. It is in Frontierland because originally this was the part of the park that prominently featured real animals.

The new Star Wars Land will cut significantly into the Frontierland that Walt built. On the northern bend of the Rivers of America will be a tall cliff of faux rocks and a series of cascading waterfalls to hide a galaxy far, far away. To accommodate the shortened river bend, certain familiar details that have always been a part of the land like a Native American village will be removed or relocated.

The love and knowledge of "cowboys and Indians" that was so prominent for the early years of Disneyland have long been replaced with an interest in "spacemen and aliens" that taps into the same fantasy of taming a wild frontier.

When Frontierland first opened it was a wilderness outpost but just like real Old West towns, it grew into a prosperous and less raucous city as it continued to expand almost immediately, with both New Orleans Square and Critter Country usurping some of its space. The entrance stockade has been remodeled twice, in 1980 and 1992, although a variety of American flags still fly along its walls.

Originally, the land was just the fort area, the riverfront (with a slight hint of New Orleans), and the Painted Desert where pack mules and stagecoaches offered guests a brief authentic experience of exploring the Wild West. Some of that same rustic spirit still infuses the land.

Big Thunder Mountain Artifacts

Big Thunder Mountain was built of steel and metal lathe covered with 9.5 acres of painted concrete, but this artificial mountain is decorated with authentic antiques.

The vintage ten-foot-tall stamp mill was built in 1880 and was trucked to Disneyland from the deserted Silver Queen Mine in California's Mojave Desert.

A stamp mill consists of a set of heavy steel stamps, loosely held vertically in a frame, in which the stamps can slide up and down. They are lifted by cams on a horizontal rotating shaft. Since the cam is on one side of the stamp, as it lifts it causes the stamp to rotate.

This is important to ensure even wear to the shoe of the stamp. As the cam moves from under the stamp, the stamp falls onto the ore below, crushing the rock, and the lifting process is repeated at the next pass of the cam.

The mill, plus tons of rock containing silver, bromite, quartz, and tungsten that make up the walls leading into the depot, were trucked from the Silver Queen Mine. Gold ore in the walls of the loading platform came from a played-out mine in Rosamond, California, which was also the setting for scenes in Disney's live-action feature film *The Apple Dumpling Gang* (1975).

There is a 1,200 pound cog wheel which was once used in the chemical breaking-down process. At the time of its installation at Disneyland, it was one of only three in existence in the world. There is a four-hundred-pound ore bucket and a hand-driven drill press. A gigantic winch motor which was converted from fuel combustion to steam power by the Imagineers is also displayed.

Giant cogs, gears, hand tools, blocks and pulleys, an alarm bell, and a dredge were also located in order to create the atmosphere of a deserted mine. All of these artifacts were specifically placed where they would be in an actual working mine.

Imagineers Pat Burke (who grew up in the Mojave Desert and explored old mines in the area) and Lee Congiardo were part of the team Disney used to locate these items to "dress the set" of Big Thunder.

The authentic cogs, gears, ore buckets, and lamps were brought in from abandoned mines and ghost towns in Nevada, Colorado, Minnesota, and Wyoming, as well as from museums, swap meets, and private donations.

Ray Bradbury Halloween Tree

On October 31, 2007, author Ray Bradbury attended the dedication of a Halloween tree at Disneyland that was to be included as part of its annual park-wide Halloween decorations. It followed a special dinner ceremony hosted by Imagineer Tony Baxter.

The Halloween Tree is a 1972 fantasy novel by Bradbury about the history of Samhain and Halloween. A group of eight boys set out to go trick-or-treating on Halloween, only to discover that a ninth friend has been whisked away and they must pursue their friend across time and space to rescue him. Along the way, they learn the origins of the spooky holiday. The Halloween Tree itself, with its many branches laden with jack-o'-lanterns, serves as a metaphor for the historical connection of these many different traditions.

An oak tree near the Golden Horseshoe Saloon was designated to be the representation of Bradbury's Halloween Tree during the Halloween season and is decorated with nearly 1,500 glowing red and orange lights and roughly 50 hand-painted jack-o-lanterns.

Bradbury, a long time Disney fan who knew Walt personally, had collaborated with the Imagineers on some Disney projects including Spaceship Earth at Epcot.

"I belong here in Disneyland, ever since I came here 50 years ago. I'm glad I'm going to be a permanent part of the spirit of Halloween at Disneyland," said Bradbury at the dedication. He would visit the tree several times before he died in 2012.

A plaque featuring some of the mask imagery from the book at the base of the tree commemorates the night of its dedication:

> On the night of Halloween 2007, this stately oak officially became "The Halloween Tree," realizing famed author Ray Bradbury's dream of having his symbol for the holiday become a part of Disneyland.

Brad Kaye, the art director for Creative Entertainment at Disneyland Resort, helped decorate that very first Halloween Tree:

> As a fan of [Bradbury's] books, it was really an honor. For the first year, [Walt Disney Imagineers] Tony Baxter, Kim Irvine, and I sat in front of the Golden Horseshoe late one night and "magic-markered" all the pumpkins. In the years following, park enhancement has done a wonderful job of keeping it up in all its Halloween glory.

During Halloween, the Disney Cruise Line ships often put up a pumpkin tree in the lobby as an homage to Bradbury's Halloween Tree.

Doritos

Just months after Disneyland opened in 1955, Frito-Lay founder Elmer Doolin opened a Tex-Mex restaurant called Casa de Fritos in Frontierland. Fritos came complimentary with every purchase.

The restaurant was hugely successful and swarmed by tourists who sought to taste "authentic" Mexican food for the first time. Casa de Fritos relocated to a larger location in 1957, in a new building designed to look like adobe, complete with faux-peeling whitewash that revealed faux brick.

Guitar players strolled the area, while servers dressed in Mexican peasant garb scurried to fill orders. In 1982, the Lawry's food empire took it over and turned it into Casa Mexicana; today, La Victoria runs Disneyland's Mexican restaurant as Rancho del Zocalo Restaurante, with a better offering of real Mexican food.

Frito-Lay didn't make the tortillas or taco shells at Casa de Fritos but contracted out to Alex Foods of Anaheim, whose factory was just about ten minutes up the street from Disneyland.

Alex Foods had a fleet of thirty-two shiny trucks that delivered tamales and other food products across southern California, along with distributing produce. It was that latter operation that resulted in the company having a contract to service many of the food venues at Disneyland like Casa de Fritos.

One day in 1960, one of the route salesmen saw discarded stale tortillas in the trash and told the cook to cut them up, fry them, and put a special blend of seasoning on them to transform them into tortilla chips which were a staple at Mexican restaurants.

Without the knowledge of the Frito company, the restaurant did it and the toasted throwaway snack became a huge hit with guests.

About a year later, while on a family vacation, Archibald Clark West, vice president of marketing for the new Frito-Lay Company, passed by Casa de Fritos and noticed customers enjoying the chips. He realized they were a happy medium between Lay's thin potato chips and Fritos' thick, curly corn chips.

He asked Alex Foods to mass produce the chips and bought all the necessary equipment. The product was named Doritos ("little golden things") and when it debuted nationally in 1966, it was a huge success.

When West died in 2011 at age 97, annual global sales of the chip (which were sprinkled on his grave by his family at the funeral) had reached about five billion dollars.

Train Station

For the Disney live-action film *So Dear to My Heart* (1949), animator and railroad enthusiast Ward Kimball researched the 1893 book *Buildings and Structures of American Railroads* by Walter G. Berg to come up with a train station for Fulton Corners. Ward liked a little antique flag depot along the Pottsville, New York, branch of the Lehigh Valley Railroad, and Walt agreed.

It was built on location at Porterville, California, as a temporary movie set and intended to be torn down once filming had been completed. Walt offered it to Kimball for his backyard railroad, Grizzly Flats.

Ward eagerly accepted the free gift, but it took him six months to painstakingly rebuild it, having to build a new frame, add an additional wall, and struggle with reassembling it piece by small piece.

Years later, when Disneyland was being built and was over budget, Walt asked Ward for the station back to use in Frontierland. Ward had invested so much time, sweat, and money to make it a real building that he refused.

Walt had the Imagineers use the original blueprints from the movie to build the Frontierland station but with some additions including a bay window, covered loading platforms on both ends, a separate freight office, and double-wide main doors to accommodate wheelchairs.

At the end of the 206-foot-long station is a genuine train-order signal from the early days of railroading given as a gift by William White, chairman of the board of the Delaware & Hudson Railroad. The signal was meant to tell engineers if there was any mail to be picked up.

In 1962, the Frontierland station was moved across the other side of the tracks to make room for New Orleans Square and in 1996 the name changed to New Orleans Square Train Station.

The sound of the clicks and clacks of the telegrapher's key in the depot originally had a more adult-oriented message but one day, while walking through the park, Walt casually mentioned that his wife Lillian had been trained as a telegraph operator. The message was quickly changed to an edited version of Walt's opening day dedication.

In the *Two Brothers* film originally shot for Epcot's American Adventure pavilion, the scene that depicts the family's Confederate soldier son returning home in a coffin to Muller's Landing was shot using this train station.

Turkey Legs

Weighing roughly one-and one-half pounds each, the infamous Disneyland turkey legs have a taste that vaguely resembles ham thanks to being cured in a similar salt-and-sugar solution. Disney has stated that the legs are meant to be shared and that the average park visitor walks about seven miles during a visit, or enough to burn off most of the calories.

Each leg is roughly 730 to 1,136 calories according to the size of the leg and weighs close to 34 ounces. The turkey legs are not unique to Disney and are sold at carnivals, state fairs, and other amusement venues around the United States.

A persistent urban myth was that they couldn't possibily be from an actual turkey and must be from another bird like an emu or an ostrich.

Keith M. Williams, a vice president at the National Turkey Federation, an industry trade group, said:

> People are accustomed to Thanksgiving turkeys, which are female birds, or hens which are traditionally much smaller; the males, called toms, are bigger—up to fifty pounds apiece—and their legs are the ones that Disney serves.

Federal law prohibits the use of steroids to make turkeys and their legs meatier. However, farmers are raising larger turkeys because of demand and so the legs are larger as well.

Turkey legs are a favorite food of Andrew Zimmern, host of Travel Channel's *Bizarre Foods*:

> I can put everyone's mind at rest. It can't be emu. I've eaten emu. It's too big, and the meat would be a little more beefy. Emu has the consistency of turkey leg but the flavor of roasted veal. It's got a mild beefiness to it and is a little more metallic.

In general, an emu leg would be about eight times the size of a turkey leg.

Marc Summers of Food Network's *Unwrapped: Walt Disney World* stated:

> Many guests aren't familiar with smoked poultry, so they pick up on the salty flavor. Disney injects their legs with a salt water cure for moisture, then smokes them. Turkey legs have pink meat because of the six-hour smoking process. It flavors the legs and keeps the inside meat pink and moist.

Disneyland sells nearly two million legs a year. In 2010, Disney created a line of merchandise souvenirs including hats, pins, magnets, t-shirts, and even air fresheners featuring an image of the item and the slogan "Nice & Juicy!"

Columbia's Maritime Museum

On July 29, 2017, the Sailing Ship *Columbia* was given a new narration and soundtrack to adjust to the changes made in the Rivers of America and surrounding area to accommodate the new Star Wars Land.

It was a trading vessel used between the U.S. and China primarily and was the first ship to circumnavigate the globe. It is also famous for lending its name to the Columbia River in Oregon. The U.S. flag on the ship's stern is the same U.S. flag that would have been used in 1787, the year the ship set sail.

Raymond E. Wallace, an architect and yachtsman who helped create the ship, explored the Pacific as a sea scout in his teens, served in the Coast Guard during World War II, and later was an officer in several yacht clubs and a board member of the Los Angeles Maritime Museum.

Admiral Joe Fowler commissioned him to do the work because Wallace had a love of classic ships. Wallace was Errol Flynn's first mate on his sailboat that they often took to Catalina. He was also responsible for the Min and Bill ship at Disney's Hollywood Studios.

A sometimes missed hidden treasure is a below-deck maritime museum first opened in 1964 in an official ceremony by former U.S. Coast Guard Admiral Alfred Carroll Richmond in full uniform to give guests a glimpse of how the ship's crew would have lived when the original ship sailed in the 18th century.

Taller guests need to mind their head as they head down the stairs into the quarters where the captain, first mate, bosun and bosun's mate, surgeon, and the rest of the crew slept and ate.

The captain's cabin is aft and is much bigger then any other sleeping quarters. He could sleep in a more comfortable bed, had a desk to write in his log, and had a small dining table. The desk includes the ship's log and letters between the captain and the ships owners. The captain also had his own windows to open and look out on the sea.

The ship's mess was in the middle forward with a pantry, and there's even a foundry to do iron work. Some of the equipment used by the crew on a regular basis is stored on this deck as well along the side walls. There is a big hatch leading to the lower storage space where cargo for the long haul could be stowed.

Fantasmic!

Fantasmic! is a twenty-five minute nighttime spectacle of pyrotechnics, lasers, water screens (30 feet tall and fifty feet wide), animation, fire and water effects, and live-action sequences featuring many favorite Disney characters and villains.

It is performed at Disneyland, Walt Disney World, and Tokyo Disneyland. All three versions have significant differences, although the basic premise remains the same. The Disneyland version was the first and debuted in 1992.

Originally, the show was going to be called "Imagination" but the Disney company found it could not copyright that title so once again created a uniquely Disney-esque word.

An updated version of the show appeared in 2017 after being closed for roughly a year and a half to accommodate the building of Star Wars Land with new state-of-the-art technology for brighter and more vibrant visuals, a re-recorded soundtrack, new choreography, and the addition of new scenes from animated classics like *Aladdin, Tangled*, and *The Lion King*. The Sailing Ship *Columbia* was no longer called into service as Captain Hook's *Jolly Roger* but was transformed into Captain Jack Sparrow's *Black Pearl*.

The opening narration sets the story for the show:

> Welcome to Fantasmic! Tonight, our friend and host Mickey Mouse uses his vivid imagination to create magical imagery for all to enjoy. Nothing is more wonderful

than the imagination. For, in a moment, you can experience a beautiful fantasy. Or, an exciting adventure!

But beware—nothing is more powerful than the imagination. For it can also expand your greatest fears into an overwhelming nightmare. Are the powers of Mickey's incredible imagination strong enough, and bright enough, to withstand the evil forces that invade Mickey's dreams? You are about to find out. For we now invite you to join Mickey, and experience Fantasmic!—a journey beyond your wildest imagination...

Mickey defeats the Disney villains who have invaded his peaceful animated dreams including the evil Maleficent who transforms herself into a massive dragon. The new version of the dragon was added in 2009 and is forty-five feet tall.

David Duffy, director of Live Entertainment for Disney, said:

> We wanted to take that original story of Fantasmic! and make it even more immersive and even more magical than it was at opening and the new technology is what allows us to do that. We wanted to make sure that we stayed true to that journey into Mickey's imagination.

Birth of Fantasmic!

The origins of Fantasmic! go back to September 1990 when Robert McTyre, vice president of Disneyland Entertainment, got a phone call from CEO Michael Eisner.

McTyre recalled:

> He [Eisner] said, "We don't have anything big and new and fabulous for Disneyland in 1992 and we need to come up with something." Basically, it was an interim step to keep interest in Disneyland high before the 1993 addition of Mickey's Toontown. We got the troops brainstorming and someone suggested a nighttime river spectacular like the IllumiNations show at Epcot."

Barnette Ricci, who directed the park's Main Street Electrical Parade for many years and created numerous other Disney live shows, was tapped to be the show's artistic creator.

Ricci said:

> We were asked to create something spectacular for Disney using the Rivers of America. We wanted something truly unique that combined a lot of spectacular effects that people hadn't seen before and with a story about Mickey Mouse that would really involve people.
>
> The core for the show was the water screens. It would be unique to project Disney animation onto one of those screens. Mickey Mouse's imagination creates these images and the audience gets involved with Mickey. We were given only twenty months, far too little time. Actually we had less than that because of the heavy winter rains earlier in 1992 that slowed things down. Doing

this complicated a show you would like to have three or four years to construct it.

To set the river on fire, a half-mile of stainless steel tubing was installed under the river. During the show, natural gas bubbles up and is ignited. The fuel shot from the Maleficent dragon contains a key ingredient. "We do it with Cremora (a coffee whitener). CoffeeMate won't work for some reason," said McTyre.

Ricci recalled:

I spent months of research studying all the Disney classics. I wanted to find just the right scenes that could be edited together successfully. One challenge was that the new lyrics had to match the mouth movements of the original animation in which characters were often saying far different lines.

We were all on graveyard shift for the last three months of rehearsal. Particularly challenging were synchronizing the movements of the performers with the computer-controlled animation and special effects. It's timed to the 30th of a second (the number of frames per second of the films being projected) and if things are two frames off, you can tell.

Orange Trees

In a 1985 interview, Bill Evans told me:

> We superimposed a drawing on an aerial photograph of Disneyland over the trees on the land and endeavored to salvage whenever possible the existing orange trees. We did this because they represented to us the equivalent of about five hundred dollars a tree which was a lot of money in 1954. Wherever the grade remained at the original elevation, we could keep the trees.
>
> If we raised or lowered the grade, we lost some trees. We opened the show with a whole lot of the original trees in place. We started with an orange grove and did selective removal.
>
> For the old stagecoach ride, we used some of the trees there. The illusion of pounding through stagecoach country was not enhanced by a crop of oranges. So we had to spend a lot of time picking all the fruit off of those trees all of the time. We did the same thing in the Jungle Ride, picking oranges off the trees to avoid the smart cracks of the ride operators who would have loved to see an orange tree when they came round the bend. We festooned those trees with all kinds of tropical vines that grew vigorously to the ultimate dismay of the orange tree hosts. All those orange trees ultimately died under the blanket of those tropical vines.
>
> Some of the walnut trees were subjected to the indignity of being truncated and inverted because Walt had another role in mind for them. We selected some because Harper Goff who was art directing the jungle had the inspiration of turning them upside down to get a kind

of a mangrove effects on to which we grafted the top half of the orange tree truncated also to get branches. It gave a pretty good illusion. I believe there are one or two left. They were cast into the concrete lining of the river.

The freeways which were penetrating the suburbs around the Los Angeles area made possible the salvage of a lot of trees that we could not otherwise have found. We literally snatched them from the jaws of the bulldozer the day before they were to be demolished. We'd box 'em out and haul 'em down to Disneyland. When I'm at Disneyland, I can tell you tree after tree. This one was from the Santa Monica freeway and that one was from the Pomona freeway and so on.

The Pope House

Owen Pope and his wife Dolly made their living exhibiting horses when in 1950 Walt Disney caught one of their shows at the Pan Pacific Auditorium in Los Angeles. In March 1951, Walt asked them to train the horses for Disneyland.

A week after Thanksgiving, Pope moved his trailer onto the Disney studio lot in Burbank, California, and the Popes became the only people to ever live there. Ten stalls were built for the horses. The Popes stayed at the studio for about two and half years with Walt visiting them every day.

Once the horses were moved to Disneyland, Owen set up loud speakers that had crowd noise and gunshots (because of the shooting galleries) cranked up to the highest volume as he trained the horses there so they could get used to the expected noise.

In addition, Pope supervised the building of Frontierland vehicles like the stagecoach and Conestoga wagon. He was also a harness maker.

As work was beginning on the construction of Disneyland, one of the houses on the land was moved to a 10-acre location behind Fantasyland dubbed the "pony farm" (and known as the Circle D Corral since 1980). The house built in the 1920s had belonged to the Witherills who were walnut growers on Harbor Boulevard. In later years it was just over the berm behind Big Thunder BBQ.

The Popes moved into the house three days before the opening of Disneyland and were the first and only people who actually resided in Disneyland. At one time, the stray dog that was the live-action reference model for Tramp from *Lady and the Tramp* (1955) lived with them as well. There were approximately 200 horses at the pony farm on Disneyland's opening day.

With the planned opening of Walt Disney World, the Popes were relocated to Florida and assisted in the development of Fort Wilderness' Tri-Circle-D Ranch. They retired in 1975. Owen passed away in July 2000 and Dolly in 2003.

The Pope House became the Disneyland credit union annex office in the late 1970s. In 1980, it was remodeled as the home for the Disneyland Media Productions office (Pony Farm Productions) and later as administration offices for the pony farm. It was relocated to a parking lot off of Ball Road in 2016 to make room for the Star Wars Galaxy Edge expansion.

New Orleans Square

Walt Disney had a special love for New Orleans. He and his wife often traveled there to purchase antiques.

While every other land in Disneyland borrowed from multiple sources, New Orleans Square is the only one dedicated to re-creating an actual city as it was at the time before the Civil War. Walt's intention until he ran out of funding to build Disneyland was to have the area at the far edge of Frontierland.

A Disneyland postcard of the area from early 1956 stated "down on New Orleans Street over in Frontierland..." Wrought-iron balconies, like those iconic of New Orleans architecture, decorated the exterior of Aunt Jemima's Pancake House and the Chicken Plantation House when the park opened.

Decorative versions of the initials "WD" and "RD" (for "Walt Disney" and "Roy Disney"), just like in New Orleans, are entwined in the railings of the second floor above the Pirates of the Caribbean because that would have been the location of an apartment suite for the brothers.

In 1959, Walt Disney met with Blaine Kern who had become an innovator in creating fanciful floats for Mardi Gras. Walt offered him a job as an Imagineer designing floats for Disneyland parades and other projects. Kern, on the advice of his boss Darwin Fenner, turned Walt down, but his work influenced the float designs of future parades.

New Orleans Square was officially dedicated on July 24, 1966, by Walt and Victor Schiro, who served as mayor of New Orleans from 1961 to 1969. The festivities included a second-line parade led by Disney and Schiro and was capped by a meal featuring "shrimp remoulade, chicken gumbo, French bread, croissants, and flaming dessert."

Walt Disney bought the elaborate chandelier that still hangs in Mlle. Antoinette's Parfumerie as a gift for his wife Lillian in New Orleans. Lillian commissioned artist Glendra von Kessel to do the mirror panel paintings for the store in a style known as "reverse painting" that had not been done in over 150 years. Glendra died before they were completed and artist Dorothea Redmond stepped in to finish them.

Both this shop and the One of a Kind Shop were designed to please Lillian's interests. She purchased in 1965 the espresso machine that is still on the back wall of Café Orleans (formerly the Creole Café). Once it was used to serve guests—including Walt himself—the popular beverage, but it is no longer in operation.

Herb Ryman: Concept Art

Imagineer Herb Ryman painted the original concept paintings for New Orleans Square including the Royal Courtyard (1962) and New Orleans Square—General View (1964). The latter painting was loaned in 1987 to the U.S. State Department's Art in Embassies program and hung in the U.S. Embassy in Paris.

In a 1988 interview, Ryman recalled:

> In that painting there is a figure that everyone thinks is me but I didn't include myself. That person was intended to be Chuck Romero, but they always come and take these things away from me before I'm really finished with them.

> Chuck Romero was an accountant who had been with the company for quite awhile. Seated near that figure is an artist wearing a beret at an easel and that was meant to be my friend [Imagineer] Colin Campbell.

> It's kind of dull just to do architecture. I try to put something personal in it. If I could have had more time, I would have put Dick Irvine, John Hench, and even Walt Disney walking around the scene.

> At the far left on the upper balcony I included the pirate Long John Silver to get the guests' attention and his movement would attract them to the building where the pirate attraction was. The nuns were the Sisters of Charity, a familiar sight in 19th century New Orleans.

> In the Royal Courtyard, the design called for the One-of-a-Kind Shop with stairs leading to the Disney family suite. I included my friend Jack Olsen, who was the first

one to see the possibility of merchandising the Disney animation cels and backgrounds.

None of us thought they were worth anything. They were going to be erased or thrown away as rubbish. Jack Olsen saw the possibility for sales and we all laughed at him like it was a big joke, but people loved them and bought thousands.

We began to call Jack the Merchant Prince. So I have a Thieves' Market and over to the far right, he's inside wrapping a package.

I was pleased to collaborate and provide some quality to Walt Disney's dreams. During my employment, I was never unfaithful to Walt's dream. I gave what I could give to Walt. One of the original designs as early as 1954 had a Dixieland band at the bend of the river and a beached pirate ship with old chests overflowing with gold, jewels, and loot as if from a foray.

Fireflies in Pirates

Fireflies, sometimes called lightning bugs, are actually a winged beetle that can produce a chemically produced bioluminescence during twilight from their lower abdomen. They are generally found in temperate and tropical climates, usually in marshes or wet, wooded areas.

Since 1967, guests have been enchanted by fireflies as they drift through the Blue Bayou at the beginning of the Pirates of the Caribbean attraction. Flitting through the reeds and cattails and helping to establish a sense of mood and place, the fireflies are an iconic part of the ride.

Screenwriter Ted Elliott mentioned that he was unable to fit a reference to the fireflies in the first film based on the attraction, *The Curse of the Black Pearl*, but they were incorporated into the subsequent *Dead Man's Chest*. They appear outside of Tia Dalma's shack.

Yale Gracey joined the Disney studio in 1939 as a layout artist working on *Pinocchio* and then later animated features including *Fantasia*. In 1959, Walt moved Gracey into WED Imagineering when he noticed Gracey spending time during his lunch hours making little gadgets and illusions.

His first assignment was to refresh some of the Fantasyland attractions, like coming up with the endless stream of tea pouring from the Mad Hatter's pot and the volcano effects in Peter Pan's Flight. Yale later admitted he had never seen a firefly in his life after he re-created the firefly effect for the Blue Bayou area of Pirates of the Caribbean.

The original fireflies were small incandescent lamps attached to thin black wires that can't be seen in the low lighting. Although the fireflies appear to "blink," they actually don't. Instead, the tiny lights are glued to black pieces of cardboard. These "flutter" due to air being blown from small fans below the flies. The blinking is therefore caused by the small light bulbs moving in and out of the guest's line of sight, creating an appearance of flashing on and off.

Today, the effect is achieved through fiber optics.

Imagineer Rock Hall told me in an interview in 2010:

> Delicate effects such as Blue Bayou fireflies were a specialty of his [Gracey's]. He constantly complained that the replacements were never done according to the original design and every time someone tried to improve on them they fouled their performance in one way or another. Yale could show you the right way to build a firefly like no one else could.

Music of New Orleans

The music of New Orleans filled Frontierland since 1955 when there was only a New Orleans-themed street at the edge of the land.

It was Walt Disney himself who created the Dixieland at Disneyland event that debuted at the Carnation Gardens on October 1, 1960, and featured big-name entertainers playing Dixieland Jazz. Dixieland Jazz is more frantic and faster than Chicago Jazz or New York Jazz. Dixieland mixes elements of military bands with street parades and adds syncopation and rhythmic swing.

The following year, in September 1961, musician Louis Armstrong joined the performances that had been moved to the *Mark Twain* steamboat. This event was filmed for the "Disneyland After Dark" episode shown April 15, 1962, on the *Disneyland* television show and later released theatrically as a short subject both domestically and overseas.

Armstrong, who was born in New Orleans, performed again in 1962 and from 1964 to 1967. In 1968, he recorded an album, *Disney Songs the Satchmo Way*, that brought the flavor of New Orleans to Disney standards. Louis Prima, the voice of King Louie in the animated feature *Jungle Book*, was also born in New Orleans.

It was not just this special event that showcased the music of New Orleans. The streets of Frontierland echoed with the sounds of the South from groups like Young Men from New Orleans (the gag being they were anything but young) who performed from 1955 to 1966.

Another group, Royal Street Bachelors, performed starting in 1966. The leader, Jack McVea, was hired by Walt himself. McVea kept the job for twenty-seven years, retiring in 1992. He was a famous musician in his own right, having written the song "Open the Door, Richard" in 1946. The original Royal Street Bachelors who all played string instruments included Harold Grant (who was replaced by Ernest McLean when Grant passed away) and Herb Gordy.

Over the decades, musical groups have included the Side Street Strutters with a horn section since 1985, and the Strawhatters.

Other groups that kept the flair alive at Disneyland's New Orleans Square were Bayou Brass (that had a Cajun flavor), Delta Ramblers, the Jambalaya Jazz Band which featured a female singer called Queenie, and the Bootstrappers, a group of singing pirates.

Pirate Skeletons

In 1995, Imagineer John Hench talked to me about the skeletons in the Pirates of the Caribbean:

> Once Walt was gone, sometimes the storytelling in an attraction wasn't as strong as it should have been. Like Pirates of the Caribbean, for instance. When you get in, you see on the door "Pirates of the Caribbean." So you expect to see pirates. Then you get on the boat, so you think: "This is okay. We're going to see pirates." The boat goes out and the first scene that you see is the restaurant.
>
> So people think: "Hey, these are not pirates. These are people having lunch. What happened to the pirates we are supposed to see?" Then we go down the chutes and it's where the pirates were. But they're all gone. There is nothing but skeletons down here!
>
> Well, it was never supposed to be like that originally. Walt died before we had finished. The original idea of Walt's was that you came down there, into the caves, and there were no pirates. ... But they had been there just seconds before!
>
> There was a hot meal on the table, steaming. There was no jewelry hidden. Walt wanted this atmosphere: they were supposed to live here; they just went outside somewhere, but they could come back at any minute and catch us.
>
> Then, you were supposed to discover the city, where they were. But because somebody liked skeletons, and that they discovered that they were [available] at a cheap price, we used too many skeletons all over the

place, and [the public] got the wrong message. Now people don't know what it was all about.

The skeletons were supposed to be at the end to show the consequences of pursuing treasure and pleasure. Nothing good is going to come of it. Learn your lesson.

Imagineers were frustrated in their attempts to create truly realistic looking skeletons so they turned to the UCLA Medical Center and obtained some real skeletons from the anatomy department. Over the years, a new generation of Imagineers replaced the real skeletons and supposedly the originals, according to former Imagineer Jason Surrell, "were later returned to their countries of origin and given a proper burial."

However, some of the originals may still remain in the attraction. Reportedly, although not officially confirmed by Disney, the skull decorating the headboard above an ornate bed is real and appears darker in color and more pitted than the fake skeletons as it has aged.

The Pirates' Redhead

For fifty years, since 1967 at Disneyland, guests have drifted by a scene where intimidating pirates are holding female captives and putting them on the auction block with a huge banner above their heads proclaiming, "Auction. Take a Wench for a Bride."

Starting in 2018, the women were no longer auctioned off. The banner was changed to read "Auction. Surrender Ye Loot." One of the most distinctive women in the scene, a self-assured redhead, became a musket-carrying pirate now called "Redd" who helped oversee the surrender of the town's "loot" with a bottle of rum at her hip.

Kathy Mangum, senior vice president of Walt Disney Imagineering, stated:

> Our team thought long and hard about how to best update this scene. Given the redhead has long been a fan favorite, we wanted to keep her as a pivotal part of the story, so we made her a plundering pirate! We think this keeps to the original vision of the attraction as envisioned by Marc Davis, X. Atencio, and the other Disney legends who first brought this classic to life.

Of course, the attraction was never meant to be historically correct. It is doubtful that pirates ever auctioned off women. It is more likely they simply took whatever they wanted by force, whether it was loot or female companionship.

Something that never occurs to guests is that the redhead is the only female with the color red in the scene.

Her clothes are more expensive, emphasizing a pronounced bust. Her hat is very stylish. She wears more make-up. She even originally had a beauty spot on her right cheek. She doesn't reflect any of the awkwardness or fear of her fellow companions.

Even the auctioneer has to reprimand her: "Strike yer colors, ya brazen wench! No need to expose yer superstructure!"

Based on Davis' original research and early sketches, she is obviously a popular and well-off lady of the night, the town prostitute, who is well aware of what her fate might be and is already negotiating to get top dollar, realizing that she is much smarter than whoever purchases her.

Marc Davis told me in a 1998 interview that he believed that after she was sold, she became a pirate herself and took over the ship. He suggested that the eye-patched woman wearing a pirate hat in the painting over the bar in the early part of the attraction was what happened to her in later years.

Dream Suite

Located at 21 Rue Royal at Disneyland's New Orleans Square, the Royal Suite (so named because the entrance was on Royal Street) was intended to be a private suite for Walt Disney and his family just above the Pirates of the Caribbean attraction. In this suite of apartments, Walt could entertain guests as well as the ten grandchildren he had by 1966 in a manner he was unable to do in his tiny apartment over the firehouse on Main Street.

The original door was located in the courtyard of New Orleans Square. It was planned that Walt's guests would climb the stairs. Walt worked with Dorothea Redmond on the overall design while his wife and decorator Emile Kuri focused on the furnishings. Walt wanted the area to be formal and elegant but still inviting.

With Walt's death in 1966, the completion was temporarily abandoned at the request of Roy O. Disney, although the infrastructure and plumbing were already in place. The living room, two bedrooms, and two bathrooms were later finished as office space.

In the first years after Walt's death, the suite was occupied by Insurance Company of North America (INA) as a VIP reception area. When INA left in 1974, Disneyland International then occupied the suite during the planning of Tokyo Disneyland with the Oriental Land Company.

When the bridge was built in front of Pirates of the Caribbean, construction was taken one step further when a pair of ornamental staircases designed by Imagineer Tony Baxter, who had designed the new footbridge, was added to either side of the balcony of the Royal Suite. The balcony window was transformed into a door, creating a new entrance to the Royal Suite, which opened as the Disney Gallery on July 11, 1987, to showcase art work and exhibits related to Disneyland, until August 2007.

For the Year of a Million Dreams promotion in 2008, the area was transformed into the Disneyland Dream Suite and restored to deluxe living quarters following the original vintage designs as well as unusual decorative items that never existed in those plans. It was used as a prize for randomly selected guests and later as special VIP lodging for celebrities and dignitaries. In 2017, it was converted into a private expensive restaurant called 21 Royal where a meal costs $15,000 for a group up to twelve.

NEW ORLEANS SQUARE

Garner Holt

In 2012, Garner Holt Productions in San Bernardino, California, acquired the complete 500,000 Disney animatronics parts inventory dating back more than forty years. Holt and his company were granted this unique honor because of their outstanding work on Disney theme park attractions as well as their commitment to innovation in building some of the most sophisticated animatronics figures ever created.

Garner Holt Productions (GHP) has over five hundred individual audio-animatronics figures in attractions at nearly every Disney theme park around the globe, from Buzz Lightyear Astro Blaster and Finding Nemo Submarine Voyage to Little Mermaid: Ariel's Undersea Adventure, the latest Matterhorn abominable snowman, and Radiator Springs Racers.

The forty-five-foot tall Maleficent dragon in the finale for Disneyland's Fantasmic! nighttime show is the work of GHP.

Holt said:

> There were delays getting it installed. You're talking about arguably the largest and most complex figure ever built.

In 1973, at the age of twelve, Holt visited Disneyland and decided he wanted to be an Imagineer. He immediately started trying to re-create Disneyland attractions in his backyard. His work received so much publicity that in 1977 he was visited by several executives from

Walt Disney Imagineering, including his personal hero, Wathel Rogers.

The Imagineers encouraged Holt to stay in school and go to college, but Holt decided to devote his time to his new company. The company evolved into providing animatronics, show action systems, special effects, and other creations for theme parks, museums, retail and dining experiences, and other attractions including Knott's Berry Farm, Universal Studios, Las Vegas resorts, and Chuck E. Cheese restaurants.

By 1997, Garner Holt Productions was being invited to be one of the bidders that the Disneyland Purchasing Department called in for their periodic new project bidder conferences. In 2001, GHP produced such animatronics as the Jack Skellington and Oogie Boogie figures for Disneyland's Haunted Mansion holiday overlay. GHP was the first outside vendor to provide audio-animatronics for Disney. They were also responsible for the Sally figure added in 2016.

GHP creative director Bill Butler said:

> Guests don't realize that ninety percent of what you see of that overlay is actually stored inside the ride during the rest of the year. If the lights were on and you could see around corners, it would be obvious. It's a huge space with lots of places to hide.

The Hatbox Ghost

The Hatbox Ghost that was installed at the Haunted Mansion on May 9, 2015, originally appeared in the attraction when it debuted in 1969 near the exit of the attic scene but was removed within weeks of the attraction's opening.

Designed by Imagineer Marc Davis and built by Imagineer Yale Gracey, he was an elderly male ghost elegantly attired in formal evening wear and with a flowing cloak and top hat and leaning unsteadily on a cane. In his other hand he clutched a vintage hatbox.

The gimmick was that his head would vanish from resting atop his shoulders and re-appear inside the hatbox with an eerie grin and then the process would reverse thanks to the wonders of black lighting. Unfortunately, the figure was installed too close to a vehicle track for it to be effective because the ambient light prevented the head from completely disappearing.

The 2015 version is a completely new audio-animatronics figure designed to look like the original. Instead of black lighting, the face is now projected onto the figure, similar to the new Constance the Bride figure. He is more expressive than the original and looks back and forth and narrows his eyes before his head dissolves into a mist and vanishes to reappear in the hatbox.

While he was removed early, he was featured on art and souvenirs and was to be a pivotal character in Guillermo del Toro's announced but never produced live-action feature film based on the Haunted Mansion.

On the storybook record, the narrator describes him as:

> He was a cloaked figure with an evil, grinning face. A hatbox hung from his hand. With each beat of his bride's heart, his head disappeared from his body and appeared in the hatbox.

What was the back story of the character? Imagineer Rolly Crump who worked on the attraction stated:

> It's always been a mystery to me. There was no continuity to the story as far as I could tell. It was all an idea here, an idea there.

Imagineer Tony Baxter said:

> It was a character that you don't see in the ride, but he was more popular than the characters that you do see in the ride. The pose told a story about something that was intriguing. If it was just a straightforward mannequin of a ghost, it'd be far less interesting than this guy hobbled over with a hatbox that has a head in it.

Critter Country

For the transformation of Bear Country into Critter Country, there was a new Br'er Bar (as a pun on the character Br'er Bear who was taking up residence in Splash Mountain) to let people know that even with the name change in the land, the bears had not vacated but were just sharing the location with some additional critters.

The sign on Pooh Corner states "Critter Country est. 1889" as a reference to the debut of Critter Country in 1989. The shop used to be the Mile Long Bar and Teddi Barra's Swingin' Arcade.

Changes were made in names to all the shops so the Indian Trading Post became the Briar Patch that featured plush toys that included a new line of characters created especially for Critter Country that Imagineer Tony Baxter hoped would be the basis for a new Saturday morning animated cartoon series.

Primarily the changes to the land were cosmetic. Hollowed-out logs doubled as makeshift houses. Tiny lanterns were added to outside burrows and tree stumps.

The landscaping of Critter Country is meant to resemble a natural backwoods area that was created by Mother Nature. For Critter Country, more than 165 trees were planted, adding to the 100 trees that were already transplanted from other areas of Disneyland. One Canary Island pine weighed over eighteen tons. The main trees in Critter Country are Monterey, Canary Island, Aleppo, and Italian stone pines, honey locust, white birch, and evergreen elm. Overgrown grasses and a large selection of shrubs add to the land's forest feel.

The back story was that the critter residents were "performing" inside the Splash Mountain attraction and so were not going to be visible to the guests who were visiting the land. However, carved wooden figures and benches decorated with the various animals would remind guests that this was the home of critters.

Imagineer Charlie Kurts, who worked on the three-dimensional designs for the attraction and the land, said:

> We don't have any critters outside their homes because we wanted the guests to have some fun guessing about them.
>
> You don't want to define everything: then there's nothing left for the imagination. I think people will get used to the new name [Critter Country]. It's really a "homey" kind of word.

Real critters also inhabit the area. Behind the Hungry Bear Restaurant is one of the secluded feeding stations for the feral cats that roam Disneyland.

Ducks at Disneyland

Guests are enthralled by the many wild ducks that inhabit the waterways of the park and who are bold enough to waddle down the walkways with baby ducklings following obediently after their mothers.

These fowl fellows are so popular that there is even an Instagram account devoted to them so that guests can document their appearances in different locations. The ducks pose in hopes that their patience will be rewarded with an edible treat.

The Complete Guide to Disneyland published by Disney in 1956 stated:

> Wild life of North America have "discovered" Disneyland. Flocks of wild geese, mallards, and other birds have found Frontierland's river a safe retreat in their pilgrimages south. The birds pause to rest here, and in some cases stay on for several months.

With a fearlessness not found in the wild, newborn offspring, accompanying their parents, wander the park, especially through the chairs and tables of the outdoor food areas in hopes of scavenging a special treat of popcorn.

Disney does try to discourage guests from feeding the wild animals, which include not just ducks but squirrels, rabbits, and other wildlife that are not an official part of the park population. As an accredited member of the American Zoological Association, Disney realizes that some foods are not always good for these animals and can actually cause digestive problems or disease that can prove fatal.

However, life is dangerous for these feathered friends in other ways as well. Feral cats patrol the park at night looking for baby ducks or duck eggs. Often, bigger birds like hawks will sit patiently and then swoop down to grab a baby duckling that has strayed a little bit too far from its flock either for itself or to feed its offspring.

Even the guests themselves can pose a threat as they gather too closely around the baby ducklings and can accidentally trample them which is why cast members often try to wrangle the ducks off of congested walkways or accompany them back to the water.

Since the ducks eat free at Disneyland, however, and are surrounded by so many others of their kind and enjoy the care that Disney takes with keeping the water clean, it seems that the advantages far outweigh the disadvantages, and that it is a bit safer than some of the other environments they might visit.

The Br'ers and the Briar Patch

The Br'er Rabbit stories contain several words that were in common usage when they were first published but may be obscure to today's readers.

In French, the term for "brother" is "frère" and a Louisiana Cajun mixture, or corruption, of both the terms "brother" and "frère" becomes "br'er," used as a title in direct address just like the term "mister."

All of the animal characters address each other by that honorific. Since CEO Michael Eisner did not want any reference to Uncle Remus in the attraction because of the possible controversy, Br'er Frog, a long-time friend of Remus, is more prominently featured.

In the *Song of the South* movie, there is a "briar patch," a "cotton patch," and even a "possum and bull patch" where possums and bulls are raised. Terms like "pumpkin patch" and "cabbage patch" to describe a specific area or a "patch of ground" used for a particular purpose have survived into present-day vocabulary usage.

The Disneyland character training department produced a video in 1976 "to acquaint you with the personality of the character" for Disney cast members who performed in costume.

One big warning in all the videos was for cast members to be careful of quick turns so that the tail did not unexpectedly hit a guest or merchandise. Originally, the characters of Br'er Fox and Br'er Bear most frequently wandered the New Orleans Square area of Disneyland but today are often found in Critter Country.

Here is an excerpt from the narration that accompanied video demonstrations of how to "animate" in the costumes:

> The stories all follow the same pattern. Crafty, high-strung, quick thinking Br'er Fox devises a perfect plan to catch the rabbit, but Br'er Bear, his well-meaning but slow-witted partner, bungles the job and Br'er Rabbit gets away. Br'er Fox goes a million miles a minute and is forever darting from place to place.
>
> Br'er Bear, on the other hand, goes half-a-mile a minute, sniffing the flowers in his own care-free way. As long as the two are together, Br'er Rabbit seems to be safe. Naturally, when one of his plans fails, Br'er Fox blames his partner.
>
> Although Br'er Bear may be simple, his temper is short and the hysterical argument usually ends with Br'er Bear bopping the fox on the head and knocking him silly. For all their foolishness, everybody loves these two inseparable comedians.

Joel Chandler Harris

On July 20, 1879, the *Atlanta Constitution* published a story written by their thirty-year-old copy editor, Joel Chandler Harris, entitled "Story of Mr. Rabbit and Mr. Fox as told by Uncle Remus."

Soon, magazines across the country were reprinting these tales which were similar to Aesop's Fables and had a moral. The first Uncle Remus book was published in November 1880: *Uncle Remus: His Songs and Sayings.*

The nine additional Remus books were collections of Harris' popular newspaper columns preserved in a more permanent format.

Harris invented Uncle Remus, a composite of almost a dozen storytellers he had heard as a young boy at the Southern plantation Turnwold. The stories had their roots in the trickster stories from West Africa and had been adapted by black slaves in the United States.

Walt Disney said:

> I first heard the stories of Uncle Remus when I was a boy down in Missouri. And since then they've been one of my favorites. I believe no folk stories have been better loved than the Joel Chandler Harris tales of Uncle Remus.
>
> It is their timeless and living appeal; their magnificent pictorial quality; their rich and tolerant humor; their homey philosophy and cheerfulness that made me want to do a picture about them.

Walt first started seriously researching the possibility of doing a feature film of the stories as early as April

1938. He bought the rights to the Uncle Remus stories from the Harris family in 1939 and, in fact, planned to make sequels if the first film was successful. Harris had died in 1908.

For financial reasons, the film is a mixture of a live-action story with Uncle Remus telling a young boy several Br'er Rabbit stories so he can learn some important lessons about life. The stories are told in animation done by Disney's top animators at the time. Splash Mountain features story elements from these animated segments.

The film was released in November 1946, but even though it took place after the Civil War, many reviewers thought it took place like other Hollywood films of the time during the era of slavery.

Disney voluntarily removed the film from being shown theatrically in the United States in 1986 because they felt the depiction of the live-action characters and the heavy use of dialect might be offensive to some audiences.

Joyce Carlson: Splash Mountain Hats

Joyce Carlson worked for the Disney company for fifty-five years in a variety of capacities, from animation to Imagineering. I did an extensive interview with her in 1998 shortly before she retired, in which she recalled:

> I used to do alot of inking on artwork for Marc Davis for some of the shows that were coming into Disneyland and for Claude Coats as well, I'd do alot of inking. So my sixteen years in the ink and paint department for animation came in handy for some of the set pieces. That was primarily for Disneyland attractions like Pirates and Haunted Mansion.

> I don't read so much any more, but if there's a certain project coming up, I'll read all about it and learn about what they want me to do. Like America Sings. That was a good show. I am sorry they removed it.

> I did all the hats for the animals, seventy-two hats. Then my boss says, "They're gonna make another set of hats" for emergency back-up. I laughed and said, "There goes another year!" It took me a full year to make all those darn hats.

> The animals later got moved over to Splash Mountain. Disney always finds a way to re-use things, but sometimes it takes us just as much money and time as if we had just built something new. Those hats on the characters shouldn't be out in all that water, because they're just glue and water themselves. They'll go limp as an old rag.

> The hats were all made of felt, glue, and water, and Marc Davis was the one that sketched them all and I had to

paint them. You go down to this place in California to get one of these hoods, where they make hats. You can't get the color of the hood, because Marc dreams up these colors, y'know.

Real nice, so I had to mix the colors. After they were hard and dried, I had like a bake shop outside the door and put them out there like cement. So I'd mix the colors, paint the hats, put the brim and crown together, and go to Pick and Save to get all these flowers to put on the hats and Marc just loved them. They were great designs and I had a lot of fun working on them.

Flash Mountain

Splash Mountain opened in July 1989. In spring 1991, a camera system was installed to take photos of the riders as they started their high speed plummet.

CEO Michael Eisner, who had been impressed with press photographs of himself riding the attraction, asked if a camera could be mounted so guests could purchase a good quality close-up picture of themselves. Amateur photographers had been frustrated since they couldn't anticipate when their friends' boat would be coming.

Disneyland vice president John Cora tested the system for several months and told the press:

> The camera will capture the image of people as they duck their heads under a mist cloud before they begin their descent.

> The image will be transmitted electronically to a video screen at the end of the ride, where guests can view the picture. If they want to buy one, a Disney employee can have one instantly printed out. We may extend it to other attractions and other parks.

The new offering was a huge success, but Disneyland did not anticipate that once guests had determined the location of the camera, and in the spirit of other outdoor amusements like Mardi Gras, that women would bare their naked breasts or others might flash a middle finger or a gang sign.

Usually, cast members were able to intercept and destroy or digitally alter the images before they were displayed to the general public, but at least one cast member posted some of them to the internet resulting in the attraction being anecdotally dubbed "Flash Mountain." An internal investigation failed to catch the culprit.

The Disney company officially owns the images but did not pursue legal action especially since the riders seem to have willingly done so and their privacy was not invaded.

In May 2009, a round of staff reductions at Disneyland resulted in the Splash Mountain photo "image screening" editor position being eliminated.

Disneyland spokesperson Becky Sanchez said:

> In evaluating the ride photo moderation role and process, we have determined that actual inappropriate behaviors by guests today are rare. Ride photos will continue to be monitored by cast members at the point of sale. In addition, the current screening system will remain intact to provide the option for management to initiate image monitoring if necessary. As always, Disneyland reserves the right to remove any visitor from the park who exhibits offensive or inappropriate behavior.

Proposing on Splash Mountain

While Disneyland executives thought it would be an inexpensive but profitable way to make some extra money when they installed a camera at the top of the flume drop on Splash Mountain to take a shot of the riders in each of the logs, they didn't realize it would inspire inventive guests to elaborately stage ridiculous photos.

It is not just inappropriate actions like showing bare breasts or flashing a middle finger that guests do for the cameras. There are shots of guests playing video games, the Monopoly board game, chess games (with the pieces glued to the board), lathering up and shaving, eating cereal, battling rubber snakes, and even marriage proposals.

In one Disneyland example, each rider held up individual signs that spelled out "Lindsay, Will You Marry Me?" and the suitor with a large picture of a diamond ring.

As one of the participants explained:

> Lindsay is, in fact, the girl in the front and she did say "yes." I would know because I was holding up one of the signs! The guy right behind her is her fiancé, Chris.
>
> I carried a backpack around all day with the signs folded up in the laptop sleeve along with snacks and jackets so she wouldn't suspect anything. The five of us behind her practiced holding the signs the day before so they wouldn't block each other from view.
>
> As soon as we were far enough on the ride, I passed out the signs (which were numbered so we had them in the right order) one by one and we hid them until we started going up the hill to the drop. As soon as we hit the

peak, we all pulled out the signs and held them up until the photo was taken, then immediately passed them to the back of the log where I re-hid them in my backpack.

She didn't see what happened because she was riding in the very front until they posted the picture on the screen at the end of the ride. The actual ring was hidden in the backpack as well to keep it safe.

As soon as we got off the ride, he gave her the ring and we purchased the pictures. We actually planned the whole thing and practiced so that it would be a complete surprise to her and pulled it off with a great picture to remember it by and a funny story to tell.

The Real Winnie the Pooh

A.A. Milne wrote a series of books about Winnie the Pooh, his son Christopher Robin (Milne), and their other animal friends in the Hundred Acre Wood. Winnie, Eeyore, Piglet, Tigger, Kanga, and Roo were based on his son's stuffed toys. Eeyore has a nail in his loose tail as he was used for "pin the tail on the donkey" games.

The characters, Rabbit and Owl, were based on animals that lived in the surrounding area of Milne's country home, Cotchford Farm, in Ashdown Forest, Sussex. It is this area on which the 100-Acre-Wood was based.

Illustrator E.H. Shepard visited the Milne family to sketch these toys "from the living model," as Milne put it, explaining:

> They were what they are for anyone to see. I described rather than invented them. Only Rabbit and Owl were my own unaided work.

Shepard may have also used his own son's stuffed animal toy bear named Growler for the Winnie design.

Christopher's mother, Daphne, bought the stuffed toy bear in August 1921 at Harrods, the famous London department store. The bear was made of golden mohair, with a black nose and shiny glass eyes. Its arms and legs were movable. Christopher initially named the bear "Edward" but later changed it to "Winnie" as a reference to a black female bear of the same name at the London Zoo that had come from Winnipeg, Manitoba, in Canada. Christopher often visited the bear, even being let into its cage to feed it honey.

The "Pooh" came from the name of a swan at the farm that was first immortalized in Milne's book of poetry *When We Were Very Young* and made Christopher laugh. Christopher recalled:

> It was my mother who used to come and play in the nursery with me and tell [my father] about the things I thought and did. It was she who provided most of the material for my father's books.

Christopher Robin's original dolls (except for Baby Roo who had been lost in a tree somewhere) insured for $50,000 were first brought to the United States in 1947 for a decade-long tour and remained in the possession of A. A. Milne's American publisher, E. P. Dutton, until their donation to the main branch of the New York Public Library. Since 1987, they have been displayed in a climate controlled case.

In 1993, the Disney company officially acknowledged that Pooh Bear was second only to Mickey Mouse in popularity, especially in merchandise sales.

Heffalumps and Woozles

Heffalumps and woozles do not appear in the original A.A. Milne books except as creatures in the imaginations of Winnie the Pooh and Piglet.

A heffalump was inspired by a young child's attempt to pronounce the word "elephant" and in the books resemble an Indian elephant. A woozle is a child's attempt to pronounce the word "weasel." Christopher Robin Milne did not have any stuffed toys of elephants or weasels.

Heffalumps and woozles are the closest thing to villains in the books and the featurettes because Pooh believes they want to steal his precious honey. Pooh gets this misconception from Tigger, a source of misinformation, who warns Pooh about their honey-stealing ways in the 1968 Disney featurette *Winnie the Pooh and the Blustery Day*.

That dire warning sparks a nightmare for Pooh where the villains appear in an homage to the iconic pink elephants on parade scene in *Dumbo* (1941). They morph into a variety of shapes, sizes, and colors accompanied by a memorable song composed by the Sherman Brothers and performed by the Mellomen.

Heffalumps and woozles were only confirmed to be real creatures in the Disney animated television series *The New Adventures of Winnie the Pooh*. A woozle honey thief named Stan and his heffalump sidekick Heff appear in the episode "The Great Honey Pot Robbery."

The Disneyland attraction references images from the original animated featurette including woozles with jack-in-the-box necks and heffalumps as hot air balloons with baskets that are honey pots.

Since the attraction was built in the same location that previously showcased the Country Bear Jamboree, the heads of three of the prominent characters from that attraction (Max the deer, Melvin the moose, and Buff the buffalo) are mounted on an archway leaving the room with the heffalumps and woozles scene. These heads are the static (non-audio-animatronic) ones from the Mile Long Bar.

With the success of the Winnie the Pooh featurettes, Disneyland considered adding a Winnie the Pooh attraction in the late 1970s. With the opening of Mickey's Toontown, there were plans for an attraction with spinning honey pots similar to the Mad Tea Party. In the mid-1990s the idea of an indoor and outdoor boat ride featuring Pooh and friends was proposed.

When both Walt Disney World and Disneyland Tokyo opened Winnie the Pooh rides, Disneyland spent over thirty million dollars to build their own version in Critter Country because there was no available space in Fantasyland.

Fantasyland

Walt Disney said:

> When we were planning Fantasyland, we recalled the lyrics of the song "When You Wish Upon a Star." The words of that melody, from our picture *Pinocchio*, inspired us to create a land where dreams come true.
>
> What youngster, listening to parents or grandparents read aloud, has not dreamed of flying with Peter Pan over moonlit London or tumbling into Alice's nonsensical Wonderland? In Fantasyland, these classic stories of everyone's youth have become actual realities for youngsters of all ages to participate in.

Walt used Fantasyland as a way to define his new outdoor entertainment venue as truly a Disney product. Disney was best known for its achievements in animation and this land showcased some of people's favorites and transported them to a real world of make-believe.

However, over the decades the land has continued to expand and change while still retaining Walt's original philosophy.

The Chicken of the Sea Pirate Ship restaurant (later called Captain Hook's Galley) that stood eighty feet tall was designed to resemble the famous *Jolly Roger* in the animated feature *Peter Pan* (1953). From 1955 until 1982, it was a Fantasyland landmark anchored in Pirate's Cove.

With the rehab of the area for the New Fantasyland in 1983, it was discovered that there was too much damage to the bottom hull to relocate it so it was demolished.

However, some of the details from the ship were relocated to the newly rehabbed Peter Pan's Flight. The ship's wheel that Peter steers in the attraction is from the famous vessel along with some of the rigging, bailing pins, and lanterns that were also salvaged.

Sleeping Beauty Castle got a face lift in 1996. The towers were repainted, each stone in the wall was re-colored, and the roof was repainted as well. Real gold leaf was added to the spires.

"The gold that we used is twenty-three carat gold leaf. It's the real deal," said Tim Deane, lead foreman of the restoration project.

Originally, individual ticket coupons were required for the attractions. For convenience, there were decorative ticket booths throughout the park for guests who needed an extra ticket. Some of those structures still survive today, although they have been repurposed. The mushroom outside the Mad Tea Party, the lighthouse by Monstro the whale, the colorful shack by the Casey Jr. circus train, and a merchandise kiosk near "it's a small world" all once served as locations to purchase additional tickets.

Disney Coat of Arms

Isgny-sur-Mer is a small village on the French coast near Normandy where Allied troops landed during World War II. From this location nine centuries earlier, French soldiers sailed to invade England and after the battles remained and established a new life. Among those soldiers was Hughes d'Isgny and his son Robert.

In that era, people were often identified by the town from where they came. So Robert d'Isgny meant it was the Robert who was from the French seacoast town. Over the decades, the name became anglicized to the more familiar "Disney."

So, Walt's ancestors came over to England with William the Conqueror in 1066, and some of them ended up holding the small village and parish of Norton Disney in the western boundary of the North Kesteven district of Lincolnshire from around the 13th century.

St. Peter's Church in the village has five monuments of Disneys (including Sir William, a knight) which have shields on them bearing three lions passant.

The "Disney window" in the church at Flintham, Nottinghamshire, has one quartering that is argent, three lions passant in pale gules.

A surname like Disney may have many different coats of arms since it was granted to an individual rather than an entire family and passed to the oldest son.

Just like at Ellis Island in America when immigrants arrived, medieval scribes in the 11th and 12th centuries often simplified or spelled names as they sounded so there were frequent variations of the name "Disney" including "Deisney."

In addition, selling family heraldry has become such a big business that some examples have been fabricated so it is problematic to determine an exact coat of arms.

According to the Disney company, the Disney heraldry is:

- Coat of Arms: Three gold fleur de lis on a red fess, representing purity or light.
- Crest: A red lion passant guardant representing bravery or courage. A crest is a part of the coat of arms.
- Motto: Vincit qui patitur (He conquers who endures).

A golden emblem of three lions passant in pale was installed on the archway above the draw bridge on Sleeping Beauty Castle sometime between the end of June 1965 and early July 1965 in connection with the Disneyland tencennial celebration. Decades later, more accurate banners were hung on the backside of the castle as well.

FANTASYLAND

Sleeping Beauty Castle

In a 1988 interview, Imagineer Herb Ryman remembered:

> [Imagineers] Marvin Davis and Richard Irvine had worked on some early concepts of the castle before I was brought in to finalize things.
>
> Walt likened the castle to a cathedral on a plain. He visualized people being able to see soaring golden towers and pennants from quite a distance. Things overpower that view of the castle these days.
>
> We were working with a limited budget when we first built it and we tried to make the most of what we had. And, as I said, we didn't have very much.
>
> Walt would have liked to have seen a castle that soared up in the sky, but it just couldn't be done at that time. The castle really needs more height to be that centerpiece, more soaring pinnacles that will go in the air giving it more vertically.
>
> By the time we did the Florida castle at Walt Disney World, we had sufficient funds. We didn't have to do a cheap castle.

Imagineer John Hench shared in 1990:

> When we were designing the Magic Kingdom for Walt Disney World, it was decided that Cinderella Castle would be more than twice the size of Sleeping Beauty Castle at Disneyland. Although Walt loved Sleeping Beauty Castle, in retrospect he thought that it should be bigger. There had been so many inquiries over the years from guests who wanted to go inside a Disney castle.

A walkthrough with ten sophisticated miniature dioramas recounting the story was opened on April 29, 1957, and dedicated by Walt and actress Shirley Temple Black who told the story of Sleeping Beauty. The dioramas were updated in 1977 (by the same team who did the Main Street, U.S.A. display windows) with miniature doll figures. The walkthrough closed in October 2001 with a new updated version based on the original designs re-opening on December 5, 2008.

In the episode "Man in Flight" (March 6, 1957) from the weekly *Disneyland* television series, Walt identified the castle as the Snow White Castle, obviously remembering a previous concept.

One of Imagineer Marvin Davis' first diagrams identifies the structure as Robin Hood's castle. In the documentary *Disneyland U.S.A.* (1956), Robin Hood and his men are sitting on the drawbridge welcoming guests into Fantasyland to tie in with the Disney live-action film *The Story of Robin Hood and His Merrie Men* (1952).

The Castle Spires

The turrets for Sleeping Beauty Castle were made out of fiberglass, at the Disney studio, and then shipped to Anaheim and assembled. It was discussed having a "camera obscura" in the highest tower, but Eustace Lycett said there was not enough light for it to be effective.

Artist Eyvind Earle, who at the time was working on the animated feature *Sleeping Beauty* (1959), told Walt that the turrets should each be different colors, like pink, red, purple, and yellow. When Walt talked with Fantasyland art director Bill Martin about the suggestion, Martin replied that he felt they should all be blue like slate because it would blend with the sky and make the structure seem taller than it actually was.

At the suggestion of Imagineer Herb Ryman, who designed the castle, Walt approved the addition of 22-karat gold leaf for the spires. It wasn't just an unnecessary ornamentation, although Walt's brother Roy thought so. Walt approved it while Roy was off on vacation.

Gold does not corrode, so it was actually a prudent financial decision in terms of preventative maintenance, especially since in 1955 gold was only about thirty-five dollars an ounce, a bargain since the price has risen several thousand percent since that time. In 1966, Walt also approved the use of 22-karat gold leaf trim for Mary Blair's façade of "it's a small world."

One unexpected detail on the castle is the Viollet-le-Duc spire, an ornate *flèche* (arrow-like spire) to the right of the tallest tower as you face the drawbridge side of the castle. While working with John Hench on Epcot in the 1970s, author Ray Bradbury noticed what he described as "a duplicate of the convoluted and beauteous spire Viollet-le-Duc raised atop Notre Dame 100 years ago" and called Hench:

> I said, "I just noticed something about Sleeping Beauty Castle. There's a spire there that I saw last on top of Notre Dame and the Palais de Justice in Paris. How long has that been there on Sleeping Beauty Castle?"
>
> John said, "Twenty years."
>
> I said, "Who put it there?"
>
> He said, "Walt did."
>
> I said, "Why?"
>
> Hench replied, "Because he loved it."
>
> I said, "Ah! That's why I love Walt Disney. It cost a hundred thousand dollars to build a spire you didn't need, eh?"
>
> The secret of Disney is doing things you don't need and doing them well, and then you realize you needed them all along.

Pinocchio Village Haus

If the 1883 children's story about Pinocchio, the little wooden puppet who came miraculously to life, is Italian, then why does the restaurant in Fantasyland resemble a medieval Bavarian building and uses the German word "haus"?

Walt Disney specifically wanted his animated feature *Pinocchio* (1940) to have the same artistic approach that echoed the Old World storybook illustrations done by German artists that had made *Snow White and the Seven Dwarfs* (1937) such a success.

For the film, concept artist Gustaf Tenggren was responsible for the design of the Alpine town in the shadow of the mountains. The Germanic influences include not only the architectural detail in the streets but also the carved interior of Gepetto's workshop. The character of Gepetto is German as are the toys, clocks, and music boxes he carves. Even actor Christian Rub who voices Gepetto was German.

Tenggren's inspiration for the buildings, signs, streets, and steps in the final film was derived from the many drawings he had done of a Bavarian town called Rothenburg ob der Tauber. Gepetto's house bears a close resemblance to the Hotel Altfrankische Weinstube in that town.

Pinocchio's Village Haus exists also at Walt Disney World and Disneyland Paris (as Au Chalet de la Marionette) and were meant to recall the classic animated feature.

For the Disneyland version, a necessary sign couldn't be centered properly above the double doors of the main exit by the construction team because of a support beam and had to be placed off center. It looked rather odd, and there was no way they could just pull it off the wall and move it as all the internal wiring had already been completed.

Since it would be time-consuming and unnecessarily expensive to fix it, Imagineer Tony Baxter came up with another idea. He climbed up on a ladder with Imagineer "X" Atencio, pencils in hand, and they drew an image of Figaro the little kitten from the Pinocchio film, pulling a rope "attached" to the exit sign.

The finished, painted graphic made it appear as if a winking Figaro was pulling the sign to the center of the wall where it belonged. When the Imagineers built the same style restaurant in Disneyland Paris, they remembered to get that exit sign right. And in celebrating the lesson learned, they painted Figaro leaning against it and giving a big thumb's up.

John Hench: Snow White Grotto

Italian sculptor Leonida Parma of the Tesconi Studio in Milan in 1958 used a popular gift box set of hand soap of the *Snow White and the Seven Dwarfs* characters released in Europe as his reference to carve the statues. Of course, in order to fit in the same size slot in the row in the box as the dwarfs, Snow White was roughly the same size as the dwarfs.

On April 9, 1961, Walt Disney along with a group of international children dedicated the Snow White Grotto and Snow White Wishing Well on the pathway to the right of Sleeping Beauty Castle. Hench's vision for the fountain was inspired by one he had seen in the small town of Brie, north of France.

In 1988, Hench recalled for me:

> I happened to be there when they were unpacking [the figures], and Walt told me to go find a place for them at Disneyland. At first I was afraid it would look like Forest Lawn and that the dwarfs had died and we'd buried them and these were the memorial markers. That's what I saw in my mind's eye.

> In fact, I told Walt that and he said, "Oh, no, no! I don't want it to look like that at all. You can figure something out to make it work."

> I told him that if we arranged them vertically that it might look all right because with the perspective [Snow White] would appear in the right proportion. He was the one who chose the path that winds around the southeast side of the castle which I think was a great choice.

The waterfall idea came along because that gave us some good excuse for grouping them vertically and having the bottom wider so the dwarfs looked smaller.

Disneyland's charm is found in the little surprises that you walk along and find. And the trick in the wishing well works particularly nicely as well to capture that unexpected extra magic. Walt hoped having the wishing well would discourage guests from throwing coins in the castle moat and could be more easily collected and donated to charity.

I thought that if we ever made another grotto area, we'd do Snow White the proper size. But the Japanese people liked it so much that they wanted it exactly the same in Tokyo Disneyland. So, everything there is exactly the same!

Exposure to the weather caused the marble to become discolored over the years and so the originals were replaced with fiberglass figures in 1983.

History of Pixie Hollow

One of the most requested characters that Disneyland park guests wanted to meet was Ariel, the Little Mermaid. Imagineers created Triton's Garden that opened officially February 1996 outside of Tomorrowland in an area that previously featured Monsanto's House of the Future and later the Alpine Garden. The area was re-classified as part of Fantasyland.

The existing infrastructure had deteriorated, so the project's art director, Kim Irvine, redesigned the walkway as a pattern of dark and light colored waves of sand-textured material, along with a green railing in a similar pattern.

Lighting for the pool was reprogrammed and a leapfrog fountain first introduced at Epcot was installed where a rod of water jumped over the walkways and re-entered the ground without a splash. 30,000 gallons of water flowed around Triton's skirt and through the trident as well as the spouts in the rocks.

Irvine said:

> Ariel is so popular, especially with the little girls. We tried to create a walk-around costume, but it wouldn't work with the tail. And Sebastian was too big. The prototype costume scared people.

> To get Ariel on stage we built a rotating clamshell throne. Ariel sits sideways on her throne, pulls her tail on, and swings around into the chair. When she is ready, the lights onstage twinkle, mist fills the air, and the shell rotates, bringing her on stage to greet the guests.

The Triton likeness had a 108-inch chest and was sculpted by Valerie Edwards using white-bearded WDI-Tujunga manufacturing technician Patrick Ivie as the model. When the area closed, the mold was used for the Triton figure for the exterior of Ariel's Undersea Adventure at Disney California Adventure.

Triton's Garden closed August 17, 2008, and in October, Pixie Hollow opened with Ariel's clamshell entrance transformed into an opening in a teapot but much of the new landscaping remaining. The story is that by walking on the pathway by an enchanted pond in a magical forest, guests are shrunk to the size of pixies surrounded by oversized blades of grass and flowers. They get to meet Tinker Bell and her pixie pals.

A Pixie Hollow video game was released September 2008 along with a straight-to-video Tinker Bell film (that made over $53 million) to support the Disney fairies pre-tween franchise across multiple lines of business that debuted 2005 and introduced new fairies who live in the fabled Neverland location.

Herb Ryman's Christmas Tree

Herb Ryman was hired by Walt Disney in 1954 to create the original overall concept drawing for Disneyland that Roy Disney used to show to investors during his initial sales pitches for the new park.

Imagineer Eddie Sotto said of Ryman:

> He understood production design and used historical context to bring real meaning to the places he created at Disneyland.

> When designing Sleeping Beauty Castle, he visited the famous Neuschwanstein castle in Germany; his visits to New Orleans during the development of New Orleans Square brought a realism to the area.

> For Ryman, it was not just "place making" but what people do in those places.

> His best-known piece of advice to beginning Disneyland designers was to make their concept art "specifically vague" so it captured the soul and emotion but left details for later.

Ryman's sister Lucille bought a three-foot-tall live spruce as a Christmas tree for Ryman to have by his bedside when he was in the hospital dying of cancer. Ryman joked he would try to outlive the tiny tree. When Disneyland horticulturist Bill Evans visited, he was amazed to see the sprouting of new shoots even though it had been kept in a darkened room.

Ryman died on February 10, 1988, and Evans arranged to have the tree transplanted to the side of Sleeping

Beauty Castle near Snow White Grotto. Ironically, it was the same location where Ryman had stood and done an interview for the Disney Channel.

After Disneyland closed one evening, several of Ryman's friends including Tim Onosko, Joen Koemmer, Frank Armitage, Larry Hitchcock, Bob Stockemer, Andrea Favilli, Tim Delaney, and Eddie Sotto gathered to dedicate the tiny tree.

The ceremony was done in secret and Ryman's friends each helped dig a hole to replant the tree. They opened a bottle of champagne to toast their departed comrade. In fact, they also buried a full glass of champagne along with the tree for Herb to join in the final toast as the sky started to mist.

The mourners threw their glasses against the side of the castle, shattering them into fragments. The original tree has died, but each time it has been replaced by a new one to honor the legacy of the man who contributed so much to the Disney theme parks, especially Disneyland. It has also been claimed the original tree was a potted pine bought by Ryman's friend John Donaldson.

Merlin's Sword in the Stone Ceremony

The walk-around costumed "face character" of Merlin from the Disney animated feature officiated the well-loved Sword in the Stone ceremony several times a day in front of King Arthur Carrousel at Disneyland.

The show began at Disneyland in summer 1983, the same year Merlin's Magic Shop closed at the park and the new architectural redesign of Fantasyland opened. The Sword in the Stone show is staged in a small circular area featuring the stone in the shape of an anvil with the sword firmly embedded. It required an electronic release from a garage-door opener.

The premise of the fifteen-minute show was that since Good King Arthur was off on vacation there was a need for a new temporary royal ruler to "safeguard and protect" the realm in his absence.

Merlin uses his magic to find the appropriate candidate with no success. Finally, Merlin picks an adult who despite his best struggles is unable to pull the sword. Then Merlin selects a child who magically raises the sword half-way and is crowned the temporary ruler. The sword only came up half-way because it was felt it was a bad idea for a child to have a dangerous sword to swing around.

Unfortunately, it took so long to find the proper ruler that his reign is already over, so Merlin gave the child a medallion and a certificate.

The text on the approximately 8x10-inch colorful certificate read:

Temporary Ruler of the Realm. Official Certificate of Coronation. Let it be know to one and all that the bearer of this certificate has been duly selected, tested, appointed and has fulfilled their duties as an official temporary Ruler of the Realm. Ceremony presided over and authenticated by Merlin, Court Wizard.

It was signed by Merlin with a star instead of a dot over the letter "i." The certificate was rolled up with a purple ribbon holding it together.

The medallion was roughly an inch and a half in diameter and less than one-fourth of an inch thick. The front of the medallion had a drawing of Wart (young Arthur) from the waist up with an extended left hand pulling the sword from the rock anvil as he looked up. On the back is the Disneyland logo, Sleeping Beauty Castle, and "The Happiest Place On Earth." It was attached to a purple lanyard.

The Matterhorn Garden

When I interviewed landscaper Bill Evans in 1985, he told me the following:

> We were allotted two weeks to complete the work on the mountain, but by the time the last artisans had cleared away their scaffolding, only three days remained until the televised opening. We installed 10,000 flowers in full bloom in those 72 hours.

> Let me tell you the prescription for planting a reproduction of a Matterhorn. The formula is to fill a steel cement bucket on the edge of a 125-foot boom with some planter mix, and then plop down a few plants and a tree and on top of the pile, plop down a gardener on top of the plants and then hoist the whole thing up in the air about a hundred feet.

> Find some place to dump the soil, sawdust, gardener, and plants, and stomp them into place. And go back down for another load. That's how the planting was done.

> The area was equipped with a plastic irrigation and drip system and some rather conventional plumbing to make sure that everything drained. We had a sophisticated system of feeding those plants. We had an old 50-foot gallon oil drum on the top of the Matterhorn connected to the irrigation system and we dumped some fertilizer in that and periodically it dribbled down on the plants.

> I think the Matterhorn was about 1/100th scale so it wouldn't do to put fir trees or pine trees up there because they would be totally out of scale. We found some old stunted pinon pines on the edge of the Colorado

Desert and brought those in. They were three to six feet high but much more in keeping with the scale. Very short needles. They are watered regularly and fed periodically with liquid nitrogen. They have been content to grow in a few shovelfuls of sawdust tucked into a pocket of concrete. But in intervals of every three or four years they get replaced.

At the base of the Matterhorn one finds an international garden. There are Colorado spruce, Chinese abelia and tallow trees, European birch, deodars from India, blue daisies from South Africa, creeping fig from Australia, sweet gum from the Gulf states, mountain lilac from California, bluegrass from Eurasia by way of Kentucky, Mexican marigold, Iceland poppy, Japanese honeysuckle, and the popular petunia that calls the whole world its home.

Mary Blair Doll

While many talented Disney artists contributed significantly to the "it's a small world" attraction, it is often considered a personal triumph for artist and innovative colorist Mary Blair who joined the Disney studio in 1940 and worked there for many years with her artist husband, Lee. She did concept art for many of the Disney films including *Alice in Wonderland*, *Cinderella*, and *Song of the South*.

She left after the completion of the animated feature *Peter Pan* (1953) and pursued a successful career as a graphic designer and illustrator including for a series of children's books. She had done some charming designs of children for the Las Posadas section of Disney's animated feature *The Three Cabelleros* (1944) and eight Christmas Hallmark greeting cards in 1945 with reproductions of her original concept art from that film.

Walt loved that appealing and distinctive look and invited her back to design the figures of the children in "it's a small world" for the 1964–65 New York World's Fair. When the attraction was moved to Disneyland, he had her design the exterior façade for it as well. A tribute to her still exists in the attraction today.

Imagineer Rolly Crump recalled:

> Mary got childlike when she designed and much of that went directly into the ride. We did a Mary Blair figure for "it's a small world" and she's still in there.

> Mary always wore wild outfits, with a poncho, and she had short blonde hair. So, we decided to include a Mary

Blair doll for the ride, with a poncho. She's standing midway up in the Eiffel Tower.

Standing halfway up on the outside of the Eiffel Tower, holding a red balloon, is the doll dedicated to Mary Blair. The little doll with short blonde hair is also dressed in Blair's quirky personal style, wearing black turtleneck, tights, boots, and a yellow poncho. Just like Mary, she has blue eyes and wears contacts rather than glasses.

During construction of the attraction for the World's Fair, Blair decorated her hard hat with flowers and glitter. For the attraction and other projects including her tile murals in the Contemporary Resort at Walt Disney World, she was assisted by Joyce Carlson who went on to supervise the installation of "it's a small world" at all other Disney theme parks. At the WDW version of the attraction, there is a doll of her instead of Mary Blair on the Eiffel Tower.

Dumbo Band Organ

With the opening of Disneyland in 1955, Dumbo the Flying Elephant was first transformed into a popular carousel-style attraction that is now located in Fantasyland at five different Disney theme parks: California, Florida, France, Japan, and Hong Kong.

Amusingly, all of the elephants on the attraction were originally supposed to be colored pink as a reference to the movie's catchy song "Pink Elephants on Parade." Walt wisely decided that guests would be happier joining tiny Dumbo himself and his clever friend Timothy Mouse instead to sail through the happiest skies on earth rather than ride an alcoholic hallucination.

In 1983, with the relocation of the attraction, Disneyland installed a vintage band organ. This mechanical marvel was built around 1915 by Gavioli, a well-known European manufacturer of circus organs. Disneyland obtained it from a pair of American collectors in the early 1970s for Bear Country.

It was never installed and was left in storage until 1982 when it was removed and refurbished for the Dumbo attraction. When Disneyland purchased it, it was in a state of disrepair due to its age and Disney craftsmen worked on it. A woodcarver along with Imagineers worked on its exterior façade. Musicians and sound technicians altered the sound system to play twenty-eight minutes of Disney songs using its wide range of musical effects.

Traditionally, band organs were meant for use at circuses, skating rinks, or wherever high-volume music was needed to attract an audience and be heard over a crowd.

The Dumbo band organ weighs three-quarters of a ton and on a clear day the music can be heard up to a mile away, so it is not frequently played.

The National Museum of American History re-opened on November 21, 2008. The east and west wings of all three exhibition floors are anchored by one of the flying Dumbo attraction vehicles to "reflect the blend of imagination, technology and business acumen that makes up American entertainment." It was donated on June 9, 2005, on the occasion of Disneyland's 50th anniversary and had been one of the vehicles on the attraction.

In the 1941 animated feature film, the name of the circus seen on a blue and pink sign on a white building as the train leaves is "WDP Circus," standing for Walt Disney Productions. Sarasota, Florida, was the winter home for John Ringling's Greatest Show on Earth beginning in 1927, which is why the WDP Circus is there as well.

Mickey's Toontown

As presented in the film *Who Framed Roger Rabbit* (1988), Toontown was both a fun and charming place ("Every Joe loves Toontown," claimed cartoon producer R.K. Maroon in the film) but potentially very dangerous for humans because the normal laws of physics, behavior, and logic were non-existent.

Toontown is mentioned in Gary K. Wolf's original novel *Who Censored Roger Rabbit* (1981) but primarily as a type of ghetto for toon characters to keep them isolated from respectable humans. Disney later used the location specifically as the home for its television show character Bonkers D. Bobcat, although it is now generally assumed that every animated cartoon character lives in Toontown.

However, it seems that Toontown is primarily the home of Hollywood cartoon characters and generally from the 1930s and 1940s. The Toontown sign on the painted hills surrounding the three acres not only provides the illusion of greater distance but is obviously a reference to the famous Hollywood sign from that same time period.

Unlike other lands of the park, there was no attempt to create a sense of reality even as Disneyland does in fantasy-like environments of the Old West or the World of the Future. Toontown is an unreal location despite the same attention to detail evidenced in the other lands.

Show director Don Carson said:

> Our initial intent was to sculpt some of the props and purchase the other ones. But because we've gone so far and so cartoony in the design, we realized no real-world item would look correct inside of Toontown. So the folks at [WDI—Walt Disney Imagineering] Tujunga and MAPO have "tooned up" 2,100 purchased props and created 958 others from scratch—picture frames, garbage cans, light switches, faucet heads. Virtually everything had to be sculpted.

Toontown was opened January 1993 to offer more room and attractions for the ever-growing attendance at the park. In order to do so, land backstage behind the berm had to be used and on nights when there are fireworks, Toontown is closed early because of its nearness to where the fireworks are launched.

WDI sculptor Valerie Edwards said:

> Toontown characters are fun and challenging to sculpt because they're based on cartoons and their proportions are different from those of reality-based figures. Translating animation to sculpture is really what we do best. That's our background.

MICKEY'S TOONTOWN

Cartoon Architecture

The challenge for Imagineers was creating an immersive environment for Disneyland guests that captured the feeling of being in the world of a theatrical animated short. Animated short cartoons feature a more distorted and fantastic fashion than the intricately detailed and subdued world of a Disney animated feature.

The movie *Who Framed Roger Rabbit* (1988) established that Toontown was a mixture of highly colorful houses and offices where everything was designed to be plausibly impossible. The emphasis was to be wild and wacky and unexpected.

Senior show producer Dave Burkhart said:

> Nothing is real in Mickey's Toontown. Everything is exaggerated. There is no conventional architecture. It's composed entirely of cartoon elements.

Senior concept designer Joe Lanzisero added:

> There is a flow and rhythm to this land you won't find anywhere else. All of the architectural elements follow certain lines, none of which are straight. There are no right angles, but there are no wrong angles either. Everything has a strong internal logic that makes sense, but it can only make sense in Toontown.

> The houses actually look—in a very subliminal way—like their namesake characters. We spent weeks in the Disney Archives and art libraries researching sixty years of cartoon history. But there was no definitive Mickey's house or Goofy's house, so it was up to designers like Don Carson, Hani El-Masri, Andrea Favilli, Jim

Shull, and Marcelo Vignali to invent them, and they went wild.

Modelmakers Jon Foster, Decio Pinto, and Todd Neubrand, among others, transformed the designers' sketches into three-dimensional models that despite their bulbous, topsy-turvy appearance had to meet the same strict building codes as the more conventional structures in the city of Anaheim.

Show designer Don Carson stated:

> The buildings are more sculptural than architectural. Conventional buildings serve as the framework. Then skins are sculpted over them to give them that fat, air-filled cartoony look.

Production designer Vern Terry added:

> These "skins" are created like rockwork, except normal rockwork cages are digitized and these are handmade. Using the drawings and models, we eyeball the framework, determine how everything's supposed to look, and then bend all the pieces, wire them on, and lay on the lath plaster base all by hand.

The final result was a unique environment that still felt familiar and accessible for guests but with an overlay of animated amusement that "draws" them in to the fun.

Interactive Community

Like its animated inhabitants, Toontown was designed to be a living, breathing, constantly changing character. It is a complete community including a downtown area with a commercial center and an industrial zone as well as a suburban neighborhood where the toons live.

All of those areas allow guests the opportunity to interact with their immediate environment with responses that sometimes change.

Production designer Ginni Barr-Ruscio said:

> It's real hands-on. Push a doorbell and you'll hear something. Turn a doorknob and it'll do something. It's non-stop. I hope kids will egg each other on to step on a manhole cover to see what it will say because there are different responses like "How's the weather up there?" or "Is it time to come out now?" We wanted the response to be unexpected so you are never quite sure what you might hear.

Producer designer Kerry Gilman added:

> The whole town is peppered with that kind of stuff. And the interactives have been programmed with random responses so one push of the plunger at the Fireworks Factory could release a dud and another could cause a hellacious explosion.

Guests can climb through rubber hose bars in the Dog Pound, activate a camera click and a bright flash of light at the Camera Shop, or create havoc of shattered panes at the Glass Factory with just a simple push of a doorbell marked "Whatever you do DON'T touch this button."

All of those interactive devices needed to be tested to not only make sure they worked consistently but could survive being touched, punched, twisted, or jumped on for over a dozen hours a day every day of the week.

Minnie's table and lamp were showcased temporarily at the Los Angeles Children's Museum to see if they could outlast the same rough treatment it might receive at Disneyland. Minnie's refrigerator has more steel than a 1968 Dodge car. Buttons, levers, and knobs had to be created to withstand millions of pushes and pulls.

Senior concept designer Joe Lanzisero said:

> You step into this magical land, let down your guard, and become a kid, no matter how old you are. You might have to bend over to get through a door or squat down to see through a window, but we have tried to make it worth the extra effort. For that day, you can be a kid in a cartoon world.

MICKEY'S TOONTOWN

Minnie Mouse's House

A major guest complaint at Disneyland was that guests weren't guaranteed an opportunity to meet Mickey or Minnie Mouse in person and snap a photo or get an autograph. In Toontown there are official meet-and-greet locations for these characters at re-creations of their houses.

Minnie's House is a purple and pink, feminine bungalow decorated with heart-shaped images. It is located next to Mickey Mouse's house. She never had a recognizable home in the cartoons or comic books, so this distinctive exterior is now considered the official design.

It appears as her home in Disney television cartoon series like *Mickey Mouse Works* and *House of Mouse* as well as the straight-to-video feature *Mickey's Twice Upon a Christmas* and video games.

The self-guided walk-through attraction includes her foyer, kitchen, bedroom, living room, and scenic backyard that includes her wishing well. A plaque states:

Welcome to my wishing well,
A secret wish you now must tell,
My reply will echo clear,
To all my friends so near and dear!

Throwing in a coin (that is donated to a local charity) or talking loudly will trigger a vocal response from Minnie herself by her official voice, Russi Taylor.

Each room has interactive features, Disney memorabilia, and displays of Minnie's belongings including many pictures and references of her sweetheart, Mickey.

In the kitchen, the Cheesemore refrigerator has a recipe for Minnie's Famous Chewy Cheesy Chip Cookies, based on a real recipe for chocolate chip cookies. However, in this version, cheese chips are substituted for chocolate chips.

Supposedly, every cheese known to "mouse-kind" is in Minnie's fridge including Jack, Bob, Mouserella, True Bleu, Gouda, Not So Gouda, and the Big Cheese.

Exiting Minnie's house out the back door, on the cupboard to the right is a book entitled "Elvis, What Happened?" Other books in her house include "A Doll's Mouse," "Little Mouse on the Prairie," "Cheese and Remembrance" (by Herman Mouse), "Ben Fur," and "Five Cheesey Pieces," among other amusing puns.

Minnie has copies of "Cosmousepolitan" magazine (spring issue). "Mademouselle" magazine, and the more risqué Jessica's Secret spring lingerie catalog.

Besides a heart-shaped mirror, and hearts on her tablecloth and welcome mat, the other primary design element is her famous bow that decorates everything, from her mailbox to her chairs.

Disneyland Rose

Walt's wife Lillian loved roses and they were prominent in her home garden.

Roses were also prominent at Disneyland since its opening. Today, the park is home to a distinctive bloom that was named after the Happiest Place on Earth. The Disneyland rose is found throughout the park as well as Disney's California Adventure but in particular in Mickey's Toontown.

Disneyland roses were first bred in the United States in 2003 by Dr. Keith Zary in conjunction with John Walden. It was introduced to the general public the following year by Jackson & Perkins. Jackson & Perkins was founded in 1872 and is a full-service nursery offering not only flowers and trees but tools, accessories, and plant-care products. It is most renowned for its 5,000 acres of rose fields and it ships over two million roses and other plants to customers every year. Disney fans can purchase a Disneyland rose from them.

This wonderful floral creation was the product of cross-breeding the Hot Tamale rose with the Sequoia Gold. The result is an extremely colorful blend of orange and pink hues on this floribunda rose. Despite its beautiful color, it has only a slight fragrance but what it does have is light and spicy. It continues to change color as it matures, so it may start out apricot or copper in color.

The blooms on Disneyland roses average about four inches or so in diameter. The blooms are somewhat full as well, with around 30–40 petals each. The plant overall is a typical size for floribundas, reaching a manageable 26–30 inches high and 20–24 inches wide, The rose is fairly resistant to many common rose diseases except blackspot. Its dark green foliage is a good contrast to its vibrant color.

These roses require a lot of sunlight, at least six to eight hours a day of full sun, though it is heat tolerant and so ideal for warmer climates. Caring for the rose is fairly easy since it requires only occasional maintenance, just generally making sure it gets enough water.

Like most floribunda roses, this variety is also a repeat bloomer. It usually flourishes from late spring to early fall and is a colorful addition to Disneyland's famed horticulture.

MICKEY'S TOONTOWN

Business as Usual

To create a sense of reality (or unreality) in a city populated by cartoon characters, Imagineers focused on the tiniest of details that are overlooked by most guests. They tried to create an environment where toons not only lived but worked and so fictional businesses were created.

Just like any city, there are service organizations that are promoted on placards at the entrance to the town. The Optimist In*toon*ational organization has a smiley face as its logo. Loyal Knights of the Inkwell and the Benevolent and Protective Order of the Mouse are also referenced. Minnie and Daisy are pictured as members of the D.A.R.—not Daughters of the American Revolution but Daughters of the Animated Reel.

Besides the obvious post office, fire station, bank, dog pound, gym, diner, fireworks factory, power house, and more, several businesses are only advertised.

One of the second-floor windows in the town is home to the Chinny Chin Chin Construction Company run by Practical Pig of the famous Three Little Pigs. ("You can't come in. Not by the hair on my chinny chin chin.") It is right next to a window for Huffin & Puffin Wrecking Company run by B.B. Wolf. (Big Bad Wolf who huffs and puffs down the pigs' houses of straw and sticks.) He is retired, according to the window.

While Gadget designed her Go-Coaster, at the attraction there is evidence on her rejected blueprints by the planning commission that Chinny Chin Chin

Construction actually built it. In Florida the construction company did the blueprints for the remodeling of the kitchen in Mickey Mouse's house but subcontracted to Donald Duck and Goofy. The name of the company could not be used in the Tokyo Disneyland version of Toontown because "chin chin" is Japanese slang for penis.

Other windows for Toontown businesses include Scrooge McDuck, Investment Counselor; Toby Tortoise, Detective Agency ("Slow & Steady Solves the Case"); Jiminy Cricket, Motivational Speaker ("No Foolin' Inc."); Singing Lessons by Clara Cluck (who often sang in Disney cartoons); and Outdoor Tours run by J. Audubon Woodlore, the Little Park Ranger for Brownstone National Park, home of Humphrey the Bear.

The only non-toon is referenced on a window above the library: "Laugh-O-Gram Films Inc. W.E. Disney, Directing Animator." Laugh-O-Gram was Walter Elias Disney's first animation studio in Kansas City, Missouri, in 1922 before he came to Hollywood. It was his first experience animating animal cartoon characters.

Talking Mickey

The first Disneyland Mickey Mouse costume that appeared on opening day in July 1955 was borrowed from the touring Ice Capades show. The costume was meant to be seen only briefly on stage and at a distance and so was designed to follow the contours of the skater's body and with a head fashioned for greater visibility.

Ron Logan, former executive vice-president of Walt Disney Entertainment said:

> Because height ranges for the characters had not been established, Mickey was sometimes over six feet tall! In the fall of 1961 that all changed through the contributions of Bill Justice and John Hench who brought a higher quality design and consistency to the characters.

Imagineer John Hench, who designed the Mickey Mouse character, stated:

> The essential characteristics that best identify the animated film Mickey and Minnie are their large heads and ears. ... Since no human body has the exact proportions that the animated characters have on screen, we had to find the right degree of exaggeration that would make the walk-around heads large enough to establish the character's identity while relating well to their body size.

Logan continued:

> In the early years, the characters walked around Disneyland freely, greeting guests and posing for pictures. There was no schedule shared with the guests, so there was no guarantee that the guests might see them. It was all serendipity, so we eventually established

a location where guests could visit with Mickey and get a photo and an autograph.

In 2010, an interactive Mickey Mouse head was introduced to the Disney theme parks where Mickey blinked his eyes, moved his mouth, and by 2013 was able to talk with guests. However, the increased costs for tech and labor compared to a "regular" Mickey became too expensive and the talking version was removed in 2018. Disney stated that just meeting Mickey Mouse was enough magic for Disneyland guests.

Without speech for decades in the park, Mickey relied on elaborate pantomime to communicate. When he became a talking character, questions arose about why Mickey didn't talk elsewhere in the park and why other characters like Minnie never talked, especially when they interacted with the talking version.

The talking Mickey costume, because it must support a head with the mechanics to move the mouth, nose, and eyes to support the illusion of speech, is heavier and wears out more quickly than a regular Mickey costume. It also requires the assistance of a backstage cast member for the proper sound.

Tomorrowland

Walt Disney said:

> Tomorrow can be a wonderful age. Our scientists today are opening the doors of the Space Age to achievements which will benefit our children and generations to come.

> In Tomorrowland, we've arranged a preview of some of the wonderful developments the future holds in store. You will actually experience what many of America's foremost men of science and industry predict for the world of tomorrow. The Tomorrowland attractions, and many others, have been designed to give you an opportunity to participate in adventures which are a living blueprint of our future.

Tomorrowland presented a constant challenge to Imagineers. As Disney landscaper Bill Evans told me in 1985:

> The decision on what plants to install in Tomorrowland was probably the most difficult facing me and my team. When Walt asked us to plant a backdrop for a tropical jungle or an arid Western desert, our direction was fairly clear and we had plenty of examples we could study. But what about plants connoting the future?

Hiding the present from the future was the ultimate goal. A new two-hundred-and-two-foot-long train station was opened in Tomorrowland in April 1958. Unlike the stations in Frontierland and Fantasyland, the station was on a raised area placed in the back so it was sometimes difficult for guests to find. Its positioning was meant to obscure the view of vintage railroad trains stopping in the future.

It was not as elaborate as the other train stations because it was supposed to represent "a futurist's design of a transport loading station" as it was described in 1958 so it was basically just a concrete block with an aluminum cover supported by tubular steel.

The large round holes in the beams were a popular "futuristic" architectural design element in the 1950s. It was a similar design to the earlier Viewliner station. Other than a new sign and new lighting installed in 1998, it has looked exactly the same for decades.

In 1998, Tomorrowland was re-imagined in the spirit of the future by looking to the past and the world of tomorrow that was showcased in magazines and movies from the early part of the 20th century in order to make the roughly five acres seem more classic rather than hopelessly outdated. The land contains more science-fiction elements than Walt had originally wanted but in so doing makes the land more timeless in its appeal.

The Redd Rockett's Pizza Port Story

Redd Rockett's Pizza Port opened May 22, 1998, in the area where the previous Rocket to the Moon/Flight to the Moon/Mission to Mars attraction had been until 1992. The food and beverage location was part of the re-imagining of Tomorrowland.

Many feel the name references both the original intention that Tomorrowland would be a space port as well as the red rocket known as the Moonliner. The Spirit of Refreshment next to Redd Rockett's features a replica of the iconic Moonliner on the roof and is fifty-three-feet high, roughly about two-thirds the size of this classic Tomorrowland landmark and roughly fifty feet from the original location of the rocket. It sits on a twelve-foot pedestal.

The Imagineers did create a back story for Redd Rockett's that appeared in *Disneyland Line* on March 27, 1998:

> By the early 21st century thousands of eager scientists, space enthusiasts and tourists were busily exploring the galaxy. Some surveyed distant planets, some worked on space stations and others enjoyed the luxury of interstellar tours. It has been decades since scientists had solved the problems of fuel and gravity...years since they had successfully re-created sunlight and oxygen. But they still had not solved the problem of good food.
>
> Space travelers loudly grumbled about the quality of space food. "It's bland. It's reconstituted. It's boring," they said. "Give us some taste!" One small colony be-

came so incensed by their meals that they ran over the cook's workstation with their T-I Probe. When asked why they did it, the colonists replied, "We couldn't stand it anymore. Just once, we wish he would have offered us a pizza."

Monitoring the exchange was an enterprising pilot and space trader, Redd Rockett. His mind froze and his eyes glazed over as he recalled the tantalizing smell of freshly baked pizza. And then, Redd came up with the perfect solution: "I'll set up a pizza port right in the middle of the sector. I'll bring the freshest ingredients and offer foods that people haven't tasted in light years!"

And so, Redd Rockett brought pizza to space travelers, along with fresh pastas, salads and desserts. Redd's original restaurant was such a hit that he soon opened a chain of Pizza Ports around the galaxy including a Tomorrowland outpost on earth. Space travelers are now content knowing that wherever they are in the galaxy, good pizza is just a shuttle away.

Secret Origin of Space Mountain

Imagineer Marty Sklar worked in different capacities in Imagineering starting in 1961 until his death in 2017.

In a 2001 interview, I asked him about his most difficult Disney theme park project. He replied:

> Most difficult project? Trying to sell RCA who was willing to put up $10 million for an attraction. John Hench and I designed a ride to go inside a computer. We pitched it to all the lower folks and finally had to make the pitch to Sarnoff [David Sarnoff, general manager of RCA].

> We put up the storyboards and we were told that Sarnoff always sat at the head of the table. So he could barely hear us and couldn't see the small storyboard drawings. He wrote a note and passed it to his vice-president who passed it to a subordinate, etc., so it eventually got to me. The note read "Who are these people?"

> Nobody had told him why we were there or what we were doing. Defeated, I told Hench to come up with a project he wanted to do and then we would try to sell RCA on it. So Hench came up with Space Mountain which was something he had been working on since 1964 with input from Walt.

> When it came time to pitch, I insisted that Card Walker and Donn Tatum accompany us, since Sarnoff knew them. Also we insisted that Sarnoff sit in the middle of the table. The RCA people said "no" and I said, "We are talking to the person sitting in that chair."

> So they put a person guarding the chair and when Sarnoff came in they said, "The Disney people would

like you to sit here." Sarnoff said, "Sure." Nobody had ever asked him before to sit anywhere else. They just assumed he wanted to sit at the head of the table.

We sold the Space Mountain project. RCA had been contracted to provide the communications hardware for Walt Disney World that had opened in 1971. Part of that contract stated they would invest ten million dollars in an attraction that interested them. RCA sponsored the construction and operating of the attraction from its 1975 debut in Florida's Magic Kingdom right up until 1993.

Over the years, we have replaced the ride vehicles, updated the technology, changed sponsorship, and made some cosmetic changes, but basically, it is still the same attraction that amazed and delighted guests and still does.

TOMORROWLAND

John Hench: Space Mountain

In an interview with me, Imagineer John Hench said:

> I had a series of meetings with Walt in 1964 about the creation of what we were calling a SpacePort. It was to be the anchor or centerpiece of the make-over of Fantasyland in 1967, but we couldn't find the funding and we were having some issues over the necessary technology for what Walt wanted.
>
> I think the original sketch for the SpacePort was done on an envelope, really. I had an idea of a type of architecture which was kind of cartilaginous. At least, that is what I called it. I worked with a sculptor named Mitsu.
>
> We built it first for Walt Disney World and the name Space Mountain came not from the attraction itself that dealt with outer space but with the mountain-like exterior. I came up with the cone shape to echo the expanding spiral of the inside track.
>
> It turned out to be a timeless design that never needed to be changed. At first, it represented what the future might be, but it evolved into becoming a fantasy of the future. The addition of music years later provided a new dimension as if the guests were riding on sound because the music was choreographed to the movement of the vehicles.
>
> The engineers had come up with pre-cast concrete and steel "T" beams for the main roof structure and traditionally, those beams would have been inside. I wanted them on the outside so that the interior was a smooth surface on which we could project images. It worked out

well because the distance between the beams start to narrow at the top so we ended up with another example of forced perspective where the building seems taller than it actually is.

Building it at Disneyland presented some challenges. While we had worked out the technology for Florida, when it came to duplicate it in California, we found that we were faced with a physical space issue. Since our original plans, there had been changes in Tomorrowland so we were constricted as to where we could put it and the Florida version was so big that it would tower above Main Street.

The solution was to reduce the intertwining double track to a simpler single track and to start construction fifteen feet below ground so the exterior looked smaller than it actually was. It took something like a thousand tons of steel when we were finished.

Edna Disney on Space Mountain

Imagineer Marty Sklar told me this story:

> Just before we opened, Edna Disney, the widow of the late Roy O. Disney, who was Walt's older brother, came down for a visit and she insisted on riding the Space Mountain attraction as we were getting set for the big premiere.
>
> She was about eighty-four years old at the time and we all tried to discourage her from riding it. Imagine the publicity of a Disney dying on a Disney attraction. But she wouldn't be discouraged and she was not the type of person you could argue with once she had her mind set. She was known for that willfulness.
>
> It only goes twenty-five to thirty miles per hour, but because it is completely dark inside, you can't see the curves or the drops so the wind on your face makes it seem so much faster. That's the illusion we worked to create and it has worked tremendously well.
>
> I distinctly remember to this day that when she got off the ride, Donn Tatum [who had become CEO and chairman of the board after the death of Roy Disney in 1971] ran up to the vehicle and anxiously asked, "Edna, Edna, are you all right?"
>
> She was annoyed and it kind of ruffled her feathers, if you know what I mean. She looked him straight in the eye and said firmly, "My sister and I used to ride all the roller coasters!" She never wanted to be treated like this fragile, helpless little thing and she wasn't. She did add that all of that was sixty years ago!
>
> Imagine that...eighty-four years old and she loved it.

John [Hench] loves telling the story of when Space Mountain first opened, he carefully watched the first guests to check their reactions. One group was some middle-aged or older ladies and they were laughing among themselves before they boarded the vehicle.

John was waiting at the exit to see if they would still be laughing at the end. When their vehicle came in, they were all dead silent and sort of stunned. One woman seemed to be hyperventilating. Another slowly got out of the car and knelt down and loudly kissed the carpet. As they made their way out the exit, they broke out into laughter again.

John feels that the reaction was that they felt that they had cheated death and that was the thrill that people get on rides like a roller coaster.

The Ever-Changing Star Tours

Ever since Star Tour's original opening in 1987, it was always the intention to continually change the attraction's film experience. In a 1987 press interview, filmmaker George Lucas stated:

> One of the basic ideas behind this is that it's reprogrammable. This will give us a big advantage in being able to upgrade the ride, to improve it or change it or make it into something else.

At the time, Lucas offered four different story choices that could be used in the future. At one point, there was so much raw material that the flight would have lasted nearly twenty minutes. There were discussions about including an underwater voyage beneath Dagobah's murky swamps or bouncing around the Star Wars universe in an out-of-control time-travel trip and even a Jedi training experience.

In 1997, Imagineer Tom Fitzgerald, one of the show writers on the original attraction, visited Lucas' Skywalker Ranch facility during post-production on *Star Wars Episode I: The Phantom Menace.* Lucas was excited about the prospect of updating the Star Tours attraction into a simulator version of the Tatooine pod race featured in that film. Imagineers even storyboarded a possible version of that race that might be used in the attraction.

However, it was decided to wait until all three films were released in order to take advantage of all the new story elements Lucas was going to introduce. In 2003, during the shooting of *Star Wars Episode III: Revenge of the Sith*, Fitzgerald met with Lucas again to brainstorm some of the possible ideas including the different locations and how things could go wrong.

The reason for the hologram transmission was to give the motion base a chance to refresh itself and reset because of the many new movements programmed into the presentation. At one point it was considered to use more live action, but the need to be able to tweak the footage and the camera angles required the majority of the film to be computer graphics. However, there are some live-action moments, like the Wookiee slamming into the windshield that was done by a stuntman.

The official storyline for Star Tours: The Adventure Continues was publicly revealed at the opening ceremonies for the attraction at Disney's Hollywood Studios in Florida on May 20, 2011. The Disneyland version of the attraction opened a few weeks later on June 3, 2011.

Star Tours: The Other Adventures

During the launch sequence for Star Tours: The Adventures Continue, guests can see other starspeeders painted with different color schemes and logos than the one they are on and an aurebesh letter emblazoned on the side of each of them for identification.

Just like the airports of today, this busy spaceport has other spacelines besides the Star Tours company using the facilities and going to other destinations. Despite the rise of the galactic empire, interstellar travel is still a thriving industry.

Those other Starspeeder 1000s that can be seen include:

- **Dantooine Express**: White with a brown diagonal at the rear with the letter "dora." Dantooine Express provides tours of the grasslands, rivers, and lakes on Dantooine, located in the Raioballo sector of the Outer Rim and far removed from most galactic traffic. On the tour, visitors see native wildlife including the kath hound, the iriaz, the kinrath, and the graul.

- **Tatooine Transit**: Solid blue with a white letter "nern." Tatooine Transit provides tours of the planet Tatooine in the Outer Rim Territories. This dangerous area is controlled by the Hutts (like Jabba the Hutt), but travelers can still visit popular sites such as Mos Espa, the Dune Sea, moisture farms, and even the infamous Mos Eisley Cantina where they may run into bounty hunters like Boba Fett.

- **Bespin Direct**: White with a brownish top and white letters outlined in red: "wesk," "dora," "isk." Bespin Direct offers tours of the gas planet in the Bespin system, located in the Outer Rim Territories. Tours include the refinery production facilities of the tibanna gas mines and the famous floating Cloud City luxury resort where Lando Calrissian is the administrator.

- **Naboo Spacelines**: Gold with a brown circle at the back with a white "nern." Naboo Spacelines travels to Naboo near the Outer Rim territories. It is a largely unspoiled world with large plains, swamps, and seas. Tours include a visit to the capital city of Theed or the underwater Gungan city of Otoh Gunga.

- **Air Alderaan**: White with a brown "aurek" letter at the back. Air Alderaan offers tours of the second planet in the Alderaan system. This planet is considered the "shining star" of the Core Worlds. Wild grasslands, old mountain ranges, and large oceans dominate the planet's land surface. One of the highlights of the tour is a visit to the capital city of Aldera.

What the Hoth?

One of the destinations that Imagineers wanted guests to visit in the updated Star Tours: The Adventure Continues attraction was the ice planet Hoth that had become such an iconic image for many Star Wars fans.

As shown in *Star Wars Episode V: The Empire Strikes Back*, the Rebel Alliance moved to the planet of Hoth after their victory in the Battle of Yavin. However, an Imperial probe droid discovered their secret base. As a result, there is a memorable battle with a herd of All Terrain Armored Transports (AT-AT), a mechanical elephant-looking vehicle sometimes referred to as Imperial Walkers, resulting in the Rebels abandoning Hoth.

Since the AT-AT attack on Hoth could not be used because it occurred much later in the timeline of the newly revised attraction, the Imagineers struggled to come up with some other appropriate adventure that could be incorporated. One scenario included wampas, the hairy white carnivorous predators that were indigenous to the planet. Another scenario included tauntauns that were used as patrol mounts by the Rebels.

Lucasfilm Ltd. and George Lucas, in particular, are well-known for being extremely protective of the Star Wars franchise, carefully reviewing everything connected with the movies, from novels to animated shows to official articles to keep the canon consistent. It was with some trepidation that the Imagineers showed the possible storylines to Lucas.

Former Imagineering senior show writer Jason Surrell recalled:

> He was very nice. He said he liked what we proposed, but he was disappointed that the adventure on Hoth didn't include the Walkers. We explained that since according to the timeline the Rebels had not yet established a base on the planet that we couldn't use them.
>
> George looked at us and said, "Who cares?" We were stunned. He explained that perhaps there was an earlier encounter with the Rebels and the Walkers on the planet while they were scouting the area. Afterward, the Rebels later decided to build a base there figuring the Empire wouldn't think the Rebels would return to that same location. He was right, of course. Guests going to Hoth would expect to see the Walkers so we added it and there have been no complaints from any of the guests who have experienced it.

Horticulture

Many of the plants in Tomorrowland are edible, like strawberries, parsley, cabbage, kale, and citrus, to represent "agrifuture" that "projects an ecologically astute future, where humanity makes the most of its resources."

More than eight hundred species of plants from more than forty nations are represented throughout the Disneyland resort. It includes approximately 17,000 trees and 100,000 shrubs. It takes approximately a 100-person horticulture staff to maintain the many acres that decorate all the different areas of the park. Trees range in size from one-foot tall dwarf spruce in Fantasyland's Storybook Land to 80-foot high eucalyptus trees in Adventureland.

Disneyland has an on-site weather responsive system to manage irrigation based on weather conditions. The system has 60,000 sprinkler heads with more than 100 satellite irrigation controllers. Low-flow irrigation systems are installed in areas throughout the resort and flow sensors and cut-off valves are used to detect leaks.

In 1985, I talked with landscaper Bill Evans who was responsible for setting the philosophy of Disneyland landscaping in 1954. He said:

> There was this one tree that had nineteen trunks. It's a palm native to West Africa. I think it is the best specimen in southern California. We found the tree up in Santa Barbara in an old estate that was about to be subdivided. We boxed that tree up. We broke all the ordinances hauling it down. It weighed twenty-two tons

and I think we got twenty-two tickets from the highway patrol. We finally got it into Tomorrowland where it remains today.

For a great many years what was good about Pershing Square in Downtown Los Angeles were these ficus trees that cast their shade on the turf of the area. The city decided they needed the space for an underground parking garage. They salvaged about two-thirds of the trees that were boxed and moved to one side. There were eight trees they decided were too big to save. They were in the process of demolishing them with a chainsaw.

I got there after they had chopped one tree down. They said they had a contract to demolish and haul them away for $150 apiece. I said, "Okay, I can top that. If you promise to take your chainsaw home and forget about demolishing them, I'll give you $50 a tree and you don't have to do any work." We went in and scooped up those trees and brought them down to New Orleans Square.

Kugel Ball

When the New Tomorrowland reopened in 1998, it was re-themed by Imagineer Tony Baxter to resemble the retro-futurist concepts that he had introduced into Disneyland Paris' Discoveryland. The challenge was always that Tomorrowland became outdated very quickly, so theming it to the imagined future made the land feel timeless.

One of the additions was Cosmic Waves, located near Honey, I Shrunk the Audience and Space Mountain. It was a series of streams of water unexpectedly spouting up from the ground surrounding a kugel ball. The goal was to avoid the fountains between sprays to get to the ball. Cosmic Waves closed in 2002 for a variety of reasons, but the ball remained.

The large granite ball floats on a thin layer of water less than the thickness of a credit card. The water, pumped from below, lubricates the stone and creates a pressure so that the solid heavy piece of stone is easily rotated.

This unique ball is not a Disney creation. Several exist in similar fountains around the world with different images including one in Walt Disney World's Tomorrowland. The term *kugel* is from the German word meaning ball or sphere.

Kusser Fountainworks of Tampa, Florida, represents the sophisticated fountain construction technology developed by Kusser Aicha Granitwerke, a leading European fountain company. This family-owned business with almost one hundred years of history is in the hands of its third generation.

In 1989, the first Kusser Fountain known as the kugel was installed in the United States. Today there are similar versions in science museums and parks.

The granite must be a perfect sphere and placed on a base that has the exact same curvature as the ball in order for the magic of physics to make it possible for even a child to move the several tons easily with a push.

The kugel ball reportedly weighs about six tons, or over 13,227 pounds, roughly the same weight as an adult African elephant. While lack of friction helps the ball to rotate, there is still some friction so the ball will not perpetually roll and guests can use their hands to stop the ball as well. Shutting off the water pressure will also stop the ball from moving.

Cosmic Waves was one of 67 pins released as a series in 1998 to commemorate some of Disneyland's favorite attractions.

Beyond the Berm

Walt Disney was always concerned that he was unable to purchase enough land when he was building Disneyland. It was one of his motivations to seek an area with enough land "to hold all the ideas and plans we could possibly imagine" in Florida.

While the berm around Disneyland shielded guests for the most part from the distractions of the outside world, especially the cheap motels that sprang up on neighboring streets, it also limited any obvious expansion. The berm ranges in height but can get up to twenty feet tall and the dirt excavated from the building of the Rivers of America was used to create that wall that surrounds the park.

At a special celebration for Disneyland cast members held at the Disneyland Hotel Magnolia Room on July 17, 1965, celebrating the park's tenth anniversary, Walt Disney complained:

> I mean when we opened, if we could have bought more land, we'd have bought it. Then we'd have had control and it wouldn't look too much like a second-rate Las Vegas around here.

When Disney ran out of room inside the berm, they cleverly expanded by putting the show buildings for the Pirates of the Caribbean and the Haunted Mansion outside the berm but with the entrances inside the berm so that guests felt they were still inside the park. The Indiana Jones show building is built on the old Eeyore section of the parking lot (and an Eeyore sign is in the attraction).

By the time of Mickey's Toontown, Disney just blatantly dug underneath the train track to reveal a new land that had supposedly always been there. The area had been used as the launching site for the Fantasy in the Sky fireworks, a small nursery, and a storage area for various large attraction props and parade vehicles.

Actually, the first Disney addition beyond the berm was a secluded enclosed picnic area to the left side of the entrance. Of course, Walt didn't want guests bringing in their own food and beverage into the park but also felt that guests shouldn't feel they were being forced into buying more expensive food in the park.

He set up a free picnic area so that guests could bring their food from home and eat there instead. It is still there today with benches, tables, and umbrella shades, near a set of lockers where guests can store their picnic goodies.

Westcot

Disney California Adventure was not the first plan for the parking lot area outside of Disneyland. In 1987, Disney executives began talking about a second gate based on elements of Florida's Epcot with construction beginning in 1992 and an opening date of 1998. The hope was to make the Disneyland area a multiple-night stay, like Walt Disney World, and to attract 25 million visitors a year.

The master plan was released to the public on May 8, 1991, but by 1995, the project was dead. Many factors were involved including expense, Anaheim not wanting to pay anything toward the building of the project, too many hotels planned, and the under-performance of the EuroDisney park.

The entrance to what was called WestCot Center featured a 300-foot golden sphere on a lush green island and an attraction inside. The silver Spaceship Earth on the other side of the country was a mere 180 feet high.

The pavilions included Wonders of Living, Wonders of Earth, and Wonders of Space. On the perimeter would be the four pavilions in the World Showcase known here as the Four Corners of the World: Asia, Europe, the Americas, and Africa. Altogether it was called the Seven Wonders of WestCot.

The Wonders of Earth pavilion would allow guests to be immersed in exotic environments, such as a jungle, the desert, underwater, or the frozen world of the Arctic. The Wonders of Living pavilion would be focused on the human mind and body and feature Body Wars, Cranium Command, Making of Me, and a different version of Journey into Imagination. Wonders of Space would feature a journey through the cosmos.

The Disneyland Hotel would undergo an extensive renovation and expansion as well. There would also be the upscale and pricey New Disneyland Resort Hotel, based on the Hotel Del Coronado, with a limited number of rooms. The 1,800-room Westcot Lake Resort would wrap around a six-acre lake with shops and restaurants.

The public esplanade would feature the Disneyland Center (shopping, dining, entertainment, like the later Downtown Disney), the Disneyland Bowl (a 5,000 seat amphitheater, much like the Universal Amphitheater), and the Disneyland Plaza (transportation hub). There would be three huge parking structures around the perimeter of the resort that featured moving sidewalks that would go to a PeopleMover system.

I'm Going to Disneyland!

Disney refers to its popular marketing campaign as "What's Next?" It is a reference to the unseen narrator's question after a major triumph where the response from the celebrity is "I'm going to Disneyland!"

The narrator is Mark Champion, a veteran radio play-by-play announcer for several football teams like the Tampa Bay Buccaneers, the Detroit Pistons, and the Detroit Lions. He got the job because a college classmate was a marketing director at Disney.

Typically, the celebrity records two different versions, one mentioning Disneyland and the other Walt Disney World. Disney gives them an "MVP" all-expense paid trip, flying them on a private jet to Disneyland or Walt Disney World, and then puts their family up in a suite for the duration of their vacation. They also are made the grand marshall of a parade and take part in various events for Disney during their stay.

As former Disney CEO Michael Eisner recalled:

> In January 1987, we were launching Disneyland's Star Tours, an attraction based on *Star Wars*. After the ribbon-cutting ceremony, my wife Jane and I had dinner with George Lucas, as well as Dick Rutan and Jeana Yeager, who had just become the first people to fly around the world without stopping.
>
> It was late and the conversation hit a lull as we waited for our food. So I asked Dick and Jeana, "Well, now that you've accomplished the pinnacle of your aspirations, what could you possibly do next?" Rutan responded,

without hesitation, "I'm going to Disneyland." And of course I go, "Wow, that's cool! You made the right choice." But my wife interjected: "You know, that's a good slogan."

Just weeks later, Disney launched the series of commercials following Super Bowl XXI on January 25, 1987. That first commercial was done by reluctant quarterback Phil Simms who was paid $75,000 (later the price was dropped for others to around $30,000) and was the MVP for the game.

Simms played for the New York Giants who beat the Denver Broncos 39-20. Broncos quarterback John Elway had been offered a similar amount of money whether his team won or lost.

Disney had produced halftime shows for the NFL and so had a good relationship with the organization and paid them for perks like being allowed on the field at the end of the game to record the statement.

Disneyland Marquee

For most people, the huge Disneyland marquee sign on Harbor Boulevard was a significant landmark announcing the entrance to the Disneyland parking lot. However, from 1955 to 1958, the sign didn't exist.

Herb Ryman had done a sketch for a sign in 1954 that featured two turrets reminiscent of Sleepy Beauty Castle and a curved ribbon banner between them stating "Disneyland Entrance," but it was never built.

According to Bill Cottrell, the first president of Walt Disney Imagineering:

> We were so anxious just to get the park opened that we didn't have the time, or probably the funds, to put much of a display out on Harbor Boulevard.

The Disneyland Hotel erected a big marquee in front of its administration building soon after it opened in fall 1955. Each letter of the words "Disneyland Hotel" was on an individual panel, with yellow panels for the "D" and "H." It seems to have been the inspiration for the similar Disneyland sign put up in 1958 that lasted for thirty years.

The Disneyland sign had a changeable marquee underneath much like at movie theaters of the time where the individual plastic letters could be changed with a long pole to provide information about Disneyland hours, off-season days closed, special events, and new attractions. An electronic marquee was installed in spring 1971.

In spring 1989, a new marquee that was thirty percent bigger (1,761 square feet) with electronic display boards to flash messages about the park and traffic instructions replaced the thirty-year-old version. It also included fiber optics so there could be color changes as well as changing the size and font of the letters.

This version was dismantled in 1999 with one side being sold to actor John Stamos and the other to collector Richard Kraft. The new version for the park was completely different since it was for the Disneyland Resort that would include Disney California Adventure and Downtown Disney as well as the Disney resort hotels, and the entrance sign reflected that new nomenclature.

Eventually, there was an ever-changing archway for different promotions but even that was eliminated in 2011 when all the traditional parking for Disneyland disappeared, so it was no longer necessary to mark the entrance in that way. Several different smaller signs are now scattered throughout the location and an homage to the original sign is on top of a waterslide at the Disneyland Hotel as well as the entrance sign to that resort.

Bill Evans and the Berm

Bill and his brother Jack did the backyard landscaping for Walt's final home in 1952 and went on to consult on the landscaping of all the Disney theme parks worldwide starting with Disneyland. I interviewed Bill in 1985:

> The purpose of the berm that wraps around the park was to exclude the freeways and the neon signs and the 20th century to which you travel in order to arrive at Disneyland. Walt didn't want that intruding on his illusions inside. So the solution was to build this berm of sand which was anywhere from ten to twenty feet high and then garnish it with all the vegetation we could lay our hands on to complete the screening and shut out the Edison transmission towers, freeway interchanges, and high-rise hotels. That back berm had some very young pine on top of it that within the first ten years grew thirty to forty feet high.

When I mentioned to Bill that I had seen an unusual picture of a machine planting the berm, he replied:

> That was a tree planting extender. That's just a plain, ordinary, garden-variety front-loading tractor, but it wouldn't reach where we had to go so we took a couple of pieces of water pipe and a chain and put a handle on the front of the tractor so we could put the trees up on the berm. In those days we didn't have hydraulic cranes that are so convenient today.

> It was characteristic that areas changed at Disneyland not excepting the berm itself. We pushed the berm aside three different times. Sort of like loosening your

belt to accommodate greater girth we had to push the railroad track out in order to let the park expand. That finally became impractical. And now, the rides penetrate the berm and railroad track. When you are in the Haunted Mansion ride or Pirates ride you are outside the railroad. The structures that house the rides were built there. You get there by going through a tunnel underneath the railroad track.

The show goes on and the trees go on, too. When we built Small World, we didn't want to lose the green tree skyline so we put the trees in boxes and put them on the roof where they are all maintained by a drip irrigation system. So the effect is when you are approaching Small World, you are seeing a continuous green backdrop even though there is a section in boxes.

Grand Californian Resort & Spa

Fringed by pine trees, this six-story resort is inspired by the 1900s Arts and Crafts design movement in California and like its counterpart, Disney's Wilderness Lodge in Florida, is meant to be reminiscent of a national parks lodge.

It is filled with one-of-a-kind art, much of which was created by artisans who were handpicked during a nationwide search. Artist Tim Burrows, who designed the Arbor Gate that leads to Downtown Disney that started as a sketch of the moon shining through the trees, said:

> I wanted to capture the feeling of the image without literally making it a tree, but still immediately be recognizable despite being somewhat abstract.

Artist Susan Dannenfelser created the tile mural of 29 bears on the front of the registration counter. Each bear, according to Dannefelser, was meant to represent a person who was involved in the resort project. The twentieth bear from the left was designated the "everyone bear."

"That way," said Dannefelser, "everyone who points to Bear 20 can say 'that's me.'" Bears six and seven represent the artist at different ages and bear eight represents her husband Kirk Beck who worked on the project with her.

Dannefelser was also responsible for the two gargoyle-like birds that stand guard by each floor of the hotel's elevator banks. The one on the third floor, because of its slicked-back feathers, was dubbed "Elvis" after singer Elvis Presley.

Flanking the elevator door openings on each floor are thick wooden shelves with some perching birds. These birds change species on each floor to reflect birds that fly higher and higher in the wild.

These are officially called the grotesque birds and are inspired by a ceramic series of the same name produced in England by the Martin Brothers between the years of 1875 and 1920. Some of the birds have removable heads because they were originally designed to store tobacco inside the bodies and so are hollow.

Real redwood paneling was used in the Hearthstone Lounge and all of the panels came from one sequoia that had died naturally. The poppies in the design on the floor of the Great Hall are closed because they are in-doors. The stained glass doors in the lobby in the closed position reveal that the two separate panels form one image of Disney California Adventure's Grizzly Peak and the resorts giant sequoia emblem.

Star Wars: Secrets of the Empire

Star Wars: Secrets of the Empire, a multi-sensory environment that combines groundbreaking technology, virtual reality, and the art of illusion, opened at Downtown Disney on January 5, 2018.

The Disney Accelerator program that started in 2014 backs around ten companies every year providing financial investment and a three-month mentorship program providing access to the Disney creative campus based in Los Angeles.

In 2017, The Void was one of the companies selected. It is a location-based entertainment company that combines interactive sets, virtual reality, real-time effects, and state-of-the-art technology to bring guests into their experiences

For the attraction, The Void also worked with Lucasfilm and ILMxLab, which is the collaboration between Industrial Light & Magic (ILM) and Skywalker Sound that's solely dedicated to creating "immersive experiences."

CEO Cliff Plumer feels that the attraction was truly a collaboration with the Lucasfilm story team:

> They spent time with us understanding our process and looking at how we go about creating our experiences, and they had a storyline in mind.

> I was fortunate enough to work with Lucasfilm on the original trilogy, and the second trilogy with George. I officially grew up with Star Wars, as did my kids. And this experience puts guests in that Star Wars universe

making choices that have consequences so each experience is different.

The official description is:

> Under the orders of the budding rebellion, your team will travel to the molten planet of Mustafar. Your mission is to recover Imperial intelligence vital to the rebellion's survival. Alongside the pragmatic droid K-2SO, your team must navigate through an enemy facility walking into danger at every turn. Disguised as stormtroopers, grab your blaster, solve puzzles, and fight giant lava monsters in an effort to fulfill your team's orders.

This story, which takes place in the same era of the film *Rogue One* (2016), features those movie cast members Alan Tudyk as K-2SO, Diego Luna as Cassian Andor, and Sam Witwer as Athex.

Each group of four guests are now Rebel Alliance operatives tasked by Mon Mothma to go undercover disguised as stormtroopers. The experience includes firing weapons, teetering near the edge of disasters, facing off with the enemy, and coming virtual-face-to-virtual-face with familiar characters. All of this is complemented by visual and auditory stimulation as well as elemental effects, such as changes in temperature, smells, air blasts, and rumbling floors.

Turtle Talk

Turtle Talk with Crush is a popular theater show that is part of Disney's Living Character Initiative program.

It opened on November 16, 2004, at Epcot's Living Seas pavilion (later renamed The Seas with Nemo and Friends). Another version opened at Disney California Adventure in July 2005. It was open briefly at Hong Kong Disneyland from May 24 to August 10, 2008. The attraction opened in Tokyo DisneySea on October 1, 2009.

Crush is a laid-back green sea turtle over 150 years old who loves riding the ocean currents and talks with the stereotypical attitude and vocabulary of a California surfer. He first appeared in the Disney-Pixar animated feature film *Finding Nemo* (2003) where he helped Dory and Marlin on their quest.

According to Crush, his father is named Mr. Turtle, so that would make Crush's full name Crush Turtle, or C. Turtle (sea turtle) for short. In the film, his voice is supplied by Nemo writer-director Andrew Stanton who recorded all of Crush's dialog lying on his couch in his office.

The show is a mixture of technologies including computer graphic techniques, image projection, digital puppetry, and improvisation. Some of the action is pre-created animated sequences that can be cued up when needed while some of the action is done in real time.

Crush is controlled on-screen in real time by a puppeteer who uses a telemetric input device similar to a keyboard so that it appears seamlessly in a virtual environment. The X-Y-Z axis movement of the input device causes the digital puppet to move correspondingly.

A talented performer behind the massive rear projection screen area that looks like a window in to the Pacific Ocean underwater environment speaks in an approximation of Crush's familiar voice and it is transferred to the speakers in the small theater.

The avatar image is projected at 60 frames per second so that the turtle's mouth is perfectly sychronized with the performer's words. The performance is a mixture of pre-scripted material and improvisational responses. Cameras mounted on either side of the screen allow the performer to see the audience and to make specific references.

In May 2016 the theme park attraction added the characters of Dory, Destiny the whale shark, Bailey the beluga whale, and Hank the "septopus" (a seven-tentacled octopus) along with Crush's son Squirt.

Walt's Garage

Just a few minutes drive from Disneyland is the location of Walt's first Hollywood studio, an old garage where he did some animation before he sold the Alice Comedies series while he was living with his Uncle Robert at 4406 Kingswell Avenue. It is located at the Stanley Ranch Museum 12174 Euclid Street, Garden Grove, California 92840.

Walt Disney's first studio in California is a one-story, two-door, one-window, all-wooden structure approximately twelve feet wide by eighteen feet long by ten feet high with lap boards and a slightly pitched roof. It was purchased from its original location by the Friends of Walt Disney for $8,500 on March 21, 1982, and later donated to the Garden Grove Historical Society for preservation.

The Garden Grove Historical Society gave the outside of the garage a new coat of white primer paint to help protect it against the weather. The inside was left untouched so that it was just as it was when Walt was inside it and dreaming of the future. Members of the Friends of Walt Disney donated some additional memorabilia to be displayed inside as well.

The official dedication of the garage was on October 20, 1984. Shortly afterwards, the Friends of Walt Disney group disbanded, feeling they had accomplished their primary goal.

Historical Society president Terry Thomas wrote:

The Disney Garage is part of our regular scheduled tours and the special group tours conducted at the museum. It is one of eight buildings currently part of the tour.

From the comments of our tour guests, it is one of our exhibits they most want to visit. We have many school and other youth groups that come and the Disney Garage is high on their list of things that they want to see.

We also have occasional visitors from all over the world drop by outside of our regular tour hours just to see the garage. We will, if possible, take the time to show it to them.

It is a very popular attraction and is one of the draws that brings the public to our museum. The Friends of Walt Disney have gone their separate ways since obtaining the garage, but their effort and personal financial investment saved a small but important structure from being demolished and gave it to the Garden Grove Historical Society for the enjoyment of the public for many years to come.

BEYOND THE BERM

Birnbaum Travel Guide

Steve Birnbaum was a writer best known for his travel commentary and guide books. He originally worked as a managing editor for Fodor's travel guides. He created his own travel guide series in the mid-1970s that totaled 36 different books from Italy to Germany to Disneyland at the time of his death from leukemia on December 20, 1991, in Manhattan, at the age of 54.

He was well known not only for his books but his appearances on television, his syndicated travel column for newspapers, and his articles in many high-profile magazines.

His wife of 31 years, Alexandra Mayes Birnbaum, continued his work including editing the Birnbaum travel guide books. The Disney books were published by Hearst while many of his other guides were published by HarperCollins. In 2001, Disney bought the brand and began publishing under its own imprint.

In 1990, as president of Disneyland and Walt Disney World, Dick Nunis wrote:

> In 1981, our company entered into a comprehensive project with Steve Birnbaum to write the first official guide to the Walt Disney World Vacation Kingdom. I was impressed that even Steve, with his acclaimed travel book reputation, would want to tackle such a project.
>
> Subsequently, Steve prepared a corresponding guidebook for Disneyland (1985), complete with numerous anecdotes and trivia, and he now updates this guide every year. I am pleased with the preciseness and quality

of Steve Birnbaum's work, which may bring some of the magic of our kingdom to you.

Birnbaum said:

> For most people in this country, Disneyland was their first experience with Walt Disney's remarkable idea of what outdoor amusement could be like. Not me. As an easterner, I had visited Walt Disney World many times before I ever made my first foray onto Disneyland's Anaheim premises, and I went with a fair amount of skepticism. After all, didn't Walt Disney World really represent [Walt's] ultimate concept? Furthermore, wasn't Disneyland just an identical copy—albeit the original one—of the Magic Kingdom at Walt Disney World? It turned out that all my doubts were unfounded, for although certain of the basics of the two extraordinary establishments are undeniably the same, Disneyland is possessed of a unique charm.

Birnbaum had access to some impressive contributors who helped him put together his guide books: John Hench, Marty Sklar, Tony Baxter, Ken Anderson, Renie Bardeau, Van France, Ron Dominguez, John Cora, Charlie Ridgway, Dave Venables, Judi Daley, and dozens of others from the Disney organization.

Famous Dignitaries

In 1965, Walt Disney told the press:

> We love to entertain kings and queens, but at Disneyland everyone is a VIP.

King Mohammed V of Morocco got a personal tour with Walt Disney in 1957, but when he arrived back at his hotel, he slipped past his bodyguards and returned to Disneyland incognito to see it again through the eyes of a typical tourist.

This gave Walt the idea for a film he was developing in 1966 where the premier of Russia, Nikita Khruschchev, did the same thing when he was not allowed in 1960 to visit the park because of concerns about security.

Here are a few of the many dignitaries who visited Disneyland during its first thirty-five years:

- King Carl XVI Gustaf and Queen Silvia of Sweden
- Prince Laurent of Belgium
- Prince Rainier III of Monaco
- Princess Caroline, Prince Albert, and Princess Stephanie of Monaco
- King Hussein and Queen Noor of Jordan
- President Sukarno of Indonesia
- Madame Jehan Sadat of Egypt
- President of the People's Republic of China Li Xiannian
- Prince Phillipe of Belgium
- Princess Anne of the United Kingdom

- Princess Margaret of the Netherlands
- Princess Sophie of Greece
- Prime Minister Pierre Trudeau of Canada
- Emperor Hirohito and Empress Nagako of Japan
- Prime Minister Jawaharlal Nehru of India
- The Most Reverend Desmond Tutu
- King Bhumibol and Queen Sirikit of Thailand
- President Mauno Koivisto of Finland
- Prime Minister David Lang of New Zealand
- Princess Haifa of Saudi Arabia
- Emperor Haile Selassie of Ethiopia
- President Anwar Sadat of Egypt
- Prime Minister of Rhodesia Ian Smith
- Duke and Duchess of Wellington
- Deputy Prime Minster of Israel Yogal Allen
- Senator Robert Kennedy, with John Glenn
- Governor George Wallace
- Senator Hubert Humphrey (who celebrated his 61st birthday in the park)
- The Mercury astronauts (for the Space Mountain opening in 1977): Scott Carpenter, Gordon Cooper, Senator John Glenn, Wally Schirra, Alan Shepard, Donald "Deke" Slayton, and Betty Grissom (widow of Virgil "Gus" Grissom).
- U.S. Presidents: Harry Truman, Dwight Eisenhower (who, along with his wife, were made honorary members of the Disneyland Fire Department), Richard Nixon, John F. Kennedy (when he was a Senator), Jimmy Carter, Ronald Reagan, and George Bush. (Lyndon Johnson never visited, but his wife Lady Bird did.)

John Hench: The Disneyland Experience

Imagineer John Hench worked for the Disney company for sixty-five years and was significantly involved in a variety of projects included the animated feature films and all the Disney theme parks.

When I asked Hench how Disney continued to build theme parks after the death of Walt Disney, he replied:

Walt did it by instinct. We do it from experience.

That experience included Hench's intensive analysis of what worked at Disneyland and why so that it could be applied in other parks. Here is an excerpt from a "brown bag" luncheon talk at Walt Disney Imagineering I attended in 1995 where he spoke about what he called the Disneyland Experience:

Disneyland was different because it was a storyboarded environment. Just like a film, everything is controlled for an audience. There are no contradictions. When there are contradictions, when there is chaos, we feel threatened.

Guests don't feel threatened at Disneyland. Guests feel reassured that there is a plan, a sense of harmony. There is nothing to fear. We toss a pseudo-menace at you now and then, but we allow you to win. You might feel you are going too fast for safety, but it really is safe and eventually, you win and you feel good about winning.

The guests experience a kind of freedom. There is a greater sense of order. At a state fair or carnival, everything clamors for you, so you look and look and try to make sense out of all these chaotic images. You are forced into making a lot of judgments.

Most people have this experience when they go to a world's fair. They walk out absolutely exhausted and they can't remember very much of what they've seen. Most of the attractions have cancelled each other out, as they were probably designed to do.

At Disneyland, when it comes to a "decision point," we try to offer only two choices. We don't give seven or eight so that you really have to work hard to decide which is the best of those choices and get mental fatigue.

We only offer two and then a little farther along, we give another two. They are still getting those seven or eight choices eventually, but we are unfolding them gradually in segments so it is less overwhelming.

We were always attempting things that would force people to move around somewhere or other and Walt would say, "Look, if they have to walk through there, you pay them for doing it somehow." You put something there that entertains or amuses or fascinates somehow.

Walt had a great affection for people and that influenced how Disneyland is designed. Disneyland is a much more pleasant experience because at least there's an attempt to relate one idea to the next.

Other parks fail at details because they are built by people who don't understand images. Images override everything.

When we began designing Disneyland, we looked at it just as we do a motion picture. We had to tell a story...or in this case, a series of stories. In filmmaking, we develop a logical flow of events or "scenes" that will take our audience from point-to-point through the story.

If we were to "leapfrog" from scene one to scene three, leaving out scene two, it would be like sending the entire audience out to the lobby for popcorn in the middle of the film. When they came back, how could we expect them to understand what's happening in the film?

There was also another thing we had to keep in mind, in further developing our Disneyland "story." In filmmaking, although we can control the sequence of events, the viewer might walk in late and through no fault of ours, miss scene one and never catch up to the story. But in Disneyland, we had more control...we designed the entire park in such a way that the guest couldn't miss scenes one or two, etc...from the minute he entered our "theater," that is, our front gate, "scene one" would begin for him.

The individual things we do in Disneyland don't have to stand as separate business entities like in other companies. We tell outsiders this and they think we're crazy, but that's the real secret to how it all works. We're looking for the total effect on the guest. That's the payoff.

There's not one thing that could be placed on the outside and stay in business. Not the Jungle Cruise...not a restaurant...and not even our popcorn machines. They are all too costly and complex. But when you put everything together, and mix in the employees, the whole effect becomes something that creates the "Disneyland Experience." Everything draws strength from other parts. It's a curious, in fact, downright incredible phenomena.

Disneyland is a virtual reality. We were doing it decades ago before all these games that kids play with today.

The Cinematic Disneyland

Disneyland is considered a theme park because it tells stories. One of the stories that Disneyland tells is that you are entering a film experience.

Outside the park, the first thing that guests see is the floral Mickey. It takes over 4,500 plants to create that familiar smiling face and it is changed several times during the year. It is one of the most photographed locations at Disneyland, second only to photos taken of Sleeping Beauty Castle.

It was Walt Disney's own idea to include this landscaped image because it was meant to resemble the same title card that appeared before a theatrical Mickey Mouse cartoon short in the 1940s and 1950s. Theater audiences would cheer and applaud when they saw it, knowing they were going to see a Disney production.

Disneyland guests are also going into a theater to see a Disney production. Along the sides of the entrance just like at a movie theater are "coming attractions" posters of things they will be seeing later. It builds anticipation.

Disneyland does not have "rides" because the word "ride" was associated with cheap and unsafe rides at carnivals, amusement parks, and fairs.

Since this is a film experience, things that might traditionally be considered rides are "attractions" to indicate the difference in quality, safety, and overall experience.

Of course, there is Mr. Toad's Wild Ride, but that name literally refers to riding in a motor car that is out of control. When Disneyland opened, cast members out of respect would refer to Walt Disney as "Mr. Disney." Walt would smile and reply, "Call me Walt. The only 'mister' here at Disneyland is Mr. Toad." Later, he would add "Mr. Lincoln" to his response.

Entering through the tunnels, one of the first things that guests smell is popcorn, a smell associated with being in a movie theater.

When you look back at the train station, it is on a hill. At the turn of the last century, all train stations were ground level because it was cheaper to build and more efficient for passengers to board.

However, Walt put the train high on a berm to block your vision so that when a guest looks back, he doesn't see the ticket kiosks or parking lot or anything of the real world. He only sees turn-of-the-last-century America.

All five of your senses are being manipulated to tell you that you are on a huge movie set representing the turn of the last century.

You hear the train. You hear its vintage bell. You hear horses clopping down the street and the putt-putt of early automobiles. You hear turn-of-the-last-century music or songs from shows like *Music Man* and *Hello, Dolly* that took place during that time period.

You smell fresh bakery goods and newly made fudge as you might have during those years. You can buy those items and taste them as well.

Items that you can touch are real wood and steel, though Imagineers made items you can't touch out of material like fiberglass. There are cast members dressed in period costumes. The buildings reflect the architecture of that time.

All of your senses are telling you that you are on a small-town Main Street at the turn of the last century. The street is transitioning your mind from the city you just came from with buildings, streets, shops, vehicles, and people to a fantasy environment of a city that is similar but is cleaner and friendlier and scaled down to a smaller size so it is less overwhelming and more welcoming.

When the park opened in 1955, each land represented the most popular movie genres:

- Main Street was the Andy Hardy films or the Frank Capra films of small towns like *It's A Wonderful Life*.

- Tomorrowland was inspired by the new science-fiction films that had begun to appear with audiences' interest in UFOs and space travel.

- Adventureland recalled not just Walt's True-Life Adventure documentaries but Tarzan movies and current television shows like *Sheena, Queen of the Jungle*.

- Frontierland was a reference to the love of westerns on television and movies like *Gunsmoke, Death Valley Days*, and *Wyatt Earp*.

- Fantasyland represented cartoons, especially the Disney animated feature films that were represented in the early attractions.

Even the newest additions are film related, with New Orleans Square relating to the Pirates of the Caribbean film franchise, Critter Country and Mickey's Toontown tapping into the Disney cartoon shorts, and the new Star Wars: Galaxy Edge into the Star Wars movie franchise.

Imagineer John Hench said:

> [Disneyland] is designed as much the same kind of thing we did in the movies but three-dimensional. We have the long-shot when you're coming in and then you see a shop and that is a medium shot and then you see some item in the window and that is a close-up. They all work together to tell the story we want to tell.

About the Author

Jim Korkis is an internationally respected Disney historian who has written hundreds of articles and over twenty books about all things Disney over the last forty years. Jim grew up in Glendale, California, where he was able to meet and interview Walt's original team of animators and Imagineers.

Jim loves Disneyland. He visited the park frequently as a child, a teenager, and an adult, and has written about its history often, including in his books *The Unofficial Disneyland 1955 Companion* and *Secret Stories of Disneyland.*

In 1995, he relocated to Orlando, Florida, where he worked for Walt Disney World in a variety of capacities including Entertainment, Animation, Disney Institute, Disney University, College and International Programs, Disney Cruise Line, Disney Design Group, Disney Vacation Club, and Marketing.

His original research on Disney history has been used often by the Disney company as well as the Disney Family Museum and other organizations.

Several websites currently frequently feature Jim's articles about Disney history:

- MousePlanet.com
- AllEars.net
- Yesterland.com
- CartoonResearch.com
- YourFirstVisit.net

In addition, Jim is a frequent guest on multiple podcasts as well as a consultant and keynote speaker to various businesses, schools, and groups.

Jim is not currently an employee of the Disney company.

To read more stories by Jim Korkis about Disney history, please check out his other books, all available from Theme Park Press.

Other Books by Jim Korkis

- Animation Anecdotes
- The Book of Mouse
- Call Me Walt
- Everything I Know I Learned from Disney Animated Feature Films
- Gremlin Trouble!
- How to Be a Disney Historian
- The Unofficial Disneyland Companion 1955
- Secret Stories of Walt Disney World
- MORE Secret Stories of Walt Disney World
- OTHER Secret Stories of Walt Disney World
- The Vault of Walt: Volume 1
- The Vault of Walt: Volume 2
- The Vault of Walt: Volume 3
- The Vault of Walt: Volume 4
- The Vault of Walt: Volume 5
- The Vault of Walt: Volume 6
- Walt's Words
- Who's Afraid of the Song of the South?
- Who's the Leader of the Club?

All books available exclusively from Theme Park Press.

About Theme Park Press

Theme Park Press publishes books primarily about the Disney company, its history, culture, films, animation, and theme parks, as well as theme parks in general.

Our authors include noted historians, animators, Imagineers, and experts in the theme park industry.

We also publish many books by first-time authors, with topics ranging from fiction to theme park guides.

And we're always looking for new talent. If you'd like to write for us, or if you're interested in the many other titles in our catalog, please visit:

www.ThemeParkPress.com

Theme Park Press Newsletter

Subscribe to our free email newsletter and enjoy:

- Free book downloads and giveaways
- Access to excerpts from our many books
- Announcements of forthcoming releases
- Exclusive additional content and chapters
- And more good stuff available nowhere else

To subscribe, visit www.ThemeParkPress.com, or send email to newsletter@themeparkpress.com.

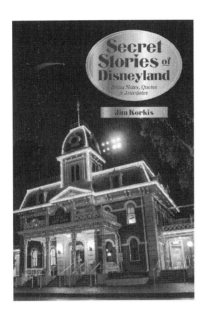

Read more about these books
and our many other titles at:

www.ThemeParkPress.com

Made in the USA
Las Vegas, NV
28 March 2021